HACKING WITH KALI LINUX

The Complete Beginner's Guide on Kali Linux and Hacking Tools.
Includes Basic Security Testing with Kali Linux, Machine
Learning, Tips and Tricks for Python Programming

By: Adam Bash

Furthermore, the information that can be found within the pages described forthwith shall be considered both accurate and truthful when it comes to the recounting of facts. As such, any use, correct or incorrect, of the provided information will render the Publisher free of responsibility as to the actions taken outside of their direct purview. Regardless, there are zero scenarios where the original author or the Publisher can be deemed liable in any fashion for any damages or hardships that may result from any of the information discussed herein.

Additionally, the information in the following pages is intended only for informational purposes and should thus be thought of as universal. As befitting its nature, it is presented without assurance regarding its prolonged validity or interim quality. Trademarks that are mentioned are done without written consent and can in no way be considered an endorsement from the trademark holder.

Table of Content

INTRODUCTION

Congratulations on downloading Hacking Tools for Kali Linux and thank you for doing so.

The following chapters will discuss in detail about hacking process in detail in a way such that people who are willing to master hacking can understand the basic methodology that hackers use along with a lot of tricks and strategies. Kali Linux is a famous operating system that is a true buddy for many hackers.

This book explains about many Linux and Kali Linux examples along with command line code that will help hackers to master their knives for an attack on the target host.

Who are hackers?

Today, the Internet plays a very important role in people's lives, work and learning. However, what followed the boom of the internet was that the security of the Internet became more and more prominent.

In the Internet, there is a class of people who have mastered superb computer technology.

They maintain the security of the Internet and some of them who are evil try to destroy it. They may damage the security of the Internet. Such people are hackers - a group that makes most Internet users awe.

Hackers are a group of people who master ultra-high computer technology. With the knowledge they have, they can work to both protect computers and network security, or to invade other people's computers or destroy the network. For hackers, what they do always has a certain purpose, perhaps for Show off, perhaps for revenge. The original intent of hackers is those who are proficient in operating systems and network technologies and use their expertise to develop new programs. What hackers do is not malicious destruction.

They are a group of technicians on the network, who are passionate about technology exploration and computer science research. In the hacker circle, the word Hack has positive meanings. For example, the system hack refers to the hacker who is familiar with the design and maintenance of the operating system; the password hacker refers to the hacker who is good at finding the user's password; the computer hacker refers to the A hacker who can make a computer obedient.

The hacker is different. The hacker refers to the person who uses the computer technology he has mastered to engage in maliciously cracking commercial software, maliciously invading other people's websites or computers. We will further discuss about the fundamental rules and things to learn before doing hacking. There are plenty of books on this subject on the market, thanks again for choosing this one!

Every effort was made to ensure it is full of as much useful information as possible, please enjoy!

CHAPTER 1:
THE HACKING PROCESS & KALI LINUX INSTALLATION

This chapter explains us about the hacking process that beginner hackers should master to get a good overview of hacking and its importance. Although being little practical this chapter will get you started and let you understand the basic things you need to know for becoming a professional hacker. We will also explain how to install a virtual machine and Kali Linux in this chapter. Let's start!

Essential things for a hacker

1) First, understand a certain amount of English:

Learning English is very important for hackers, because most of the materials and tutorials are now in English. Therefore, learning hackers should try to read English materials, use English software, and pay attention to famous foreign network security websites in time. You may occasionally use foreign resources to master hacking methods and techniques.

2) *Second, learn the use of basic software:*

The basic software mentioned here refers to two contents. One is the common computer commands we use every day, such as ftp, ping, net, etc.; on the other hand, we must learn about hacking tools. This mainly includes port scanners, vulnerability scanners, information interception tools and password cracking tools. Because these software's have many varieties and different functions, this book will introduce several popular software usage methods. After learning the basic principles, learners can choose either their own tools or create their own tools. Find the development guide for the software and write your own hacking tools for a better understanding of the network structure.

3) *Third, a preliminary understanding of the network protocol and working principle:*

The so-called "preliminary understanding" is to "get their own understanding on the topic" to understand the working principle of the network, because the knowledge involved in the agreement is complex and complex, so if you conduct in-depth research at the beginning, it is bound to Will greatly dampen the enthusiasm for learning. Here I suggest that learners have a preliminary understanding of the TCP/IP protocol, especially how the network communicates and how information is exchanged when browsing the web, how the client browser applies for "handshake information", how the server "responses to handshake information" and "accepts requests".

4) Get Familiar with several popular programming languages and scripts:

As mentioned above, there is no requirement for learners to learn in depth, as long as they can understand the language and know the results of the program execution. It is recommended that learners initially learn python language, asp and cgi scripting language, and do basic understanding of html hypertext language and php, java, etc., you need to concentrate mainly on the "variables" and "array" parts of these languages, because there is an inherent connection between languages. In a way such that so as long as you are proficient in one of them, other languages can be the same, it is recommended to learn C language and html hypertext language.

5) *Get Familiar with web applications:*

Web applications include various server software daemons, such as wuftp, Apache and other server backgrounds. There are various popular forums and e-communities on the Internet. Conditional learners should make their own computers into servers, and then install and run some forum code. After some trials, they will be sensible to understand the working principle of the network, which is much easier than relying on theoretical learning. Try to do more with less work.

Some important concepts you need to master before hacking:

1. *The Protocol*

Network is a place for information exchange. All computers accessing the network can exchange information through physical connection between devices. Physical equipment includes the most common cables, optical cables, wireless WAPs, and microwaves. However, simply possessing these physical devices does not enable the exchange of information. It is as if the human body cannot be dominated by the brain, and the information exchange must have a software environment. This software environment is a set of rules that humans have implemented.

It is called a "protocol. With a protocol, different computers can use physical devices in accordance with the same protocol, and do not cause mutual incomprehension.

This kind of agreement is very similar to Morse code. It can be changed in a simple way. However, if there is no control table, no one can understand what the content of a chaotic code is. The same is true for computers, which accomplish different missions through various pre-defined protocols. For example, the RFC1459 protocol enables IRC servers to communicate with client computers. Therefore, both hackers and network administrators must achieve the purpose of understanding the network operation mechanism through learning protocols.

Each protocol has been modified and used for many years. The newly generated protocols are mostly established based on the basic protocol. Therefore, the basic protocol has a relatively high security mechanism. It is difficult for hackers to discover the security problems in the protocol. However, for some new types of protocols, because of a short time and poor consideration, they may also be exploited by hackers for security reasons.

For the discussion of network protocols, more people think that the basic protocol used today has security risks at the beginning of design. Therefore, no matter what changes are made to the network, as long as the network system does not undergo fundamental changes, it is fundamentally impossible to prevent the emergence of cyber hackers. This kind of hacking function is beyond the scope of this book, so it is not covered here.

2. The server and the client:

The simplest form of network service is several computers as clients, using one computer as a server where each client has the ability to make requests to the server, then the server responds and completes the requested action, and finally the server will return the execution result to the client computer. There are many such agreements. For example, the email server, web server, chat room server, etc. that we usually contact is all of this type. There is also a connection method, which does not require server support, but directly connects two client computers, which means that each computer is both a server and a client, and they have the same function.

Peer-to-peer completion of the connection and information exchange work. For example, the DCC transmission protocol falls into this category.

It can be seen from this that the client and the server are the requesting application computer and the answering computer specified in various protocols, respectively. As a general Internet user, they all operate their own computers (clients), and send regular requests to the web server to complete actions such as browsing the web, sending and receiving emails, and for hackers through their own computers (The client) attacks other computers (which may be clients or servers) to invade, destroy, and steal information.

3. The system and system environment:

Operating system must be installed to operate the computer. The popular operating system is mainly UNIX, Linux, Mac, BSD, Windows2000, Windows95/98/Me, Windows NT, etc., these operating systems run independently and has its own file management, memory management, process management and other mechanisms. On the network, these different operating systems can be operated as servers or as clients, and they can exchange information through the protocol jobs.

Different operating systems and different applications constitute the system environment. For example, the Linux system can be used to configure the computer as a web server with Apache software. Other computers using the client can use the browser to obtain the website server for the viewer to read. The text information as Windows 2000 with Ftp software can be set up as a file server, through remote ftp login and can get various file resources on the system.

4. IP address and port:

We go online and browse the web at the same time, send and receive e-mail, voice chat and So many network service projects are completed through different protocols, but the network is so big than our computer. How can I find the computer I need for my service? How to do so much work on one computer at the same time? Here we will introduce the IP address. Every computer that is connected to the Internet has a unique IP address. This address is similar to the home address of people in the world. Through a variety of physical devices such as network routers (without the need for beginners to understand), the network can complete from one computer to another.

The exchange of information between the works, because their IP addresses are different, so there will be no confusion that cannot find the target. However, hackers can forge their own computer's IP address through special methods, so that when the server receives a request from a hacker computer (pseudo IP address), the server will send the response message to the pseudo IP address, causing network confusion. Of course, hackers can easily find any surfers or servers based on IP addresses and attack them (think of real-time burglary).

Next, I will explain the second question mentioned above: Why can I use multiple network services at the same time on one computer? It seems that New York City has eight gates. Different protocols are reflected in different network services, and different network services will open different ports (City Gates) on the client computer to complete its information transmission. Of course, if a web server has multiple network services open at the same time, it also has to open a number of different ports (city gates) to accommodate different client requests.

The back door that is often heard on the Internet means that the hacker has opened up a network service on the server through special functions. This service can be used to specifically complete the purpose of the hacker and then the server will be opened with a new port. This kind of service, because hackers use this port, it is easy to be discovered by ordinary Internet users and network administrators, that is, "hidden ports", so a back door is created.

Each computer can open 65,535 ports, so in theory, we can develop at least 65,535 different network services, but in fact, this number is very large. The network often uses dozens of service agreements, such as browsing web clients. Both port and server use port 80. For IRC chat, port 6667 is used on the server and port 1026 is used on the client.

5. Vulnerabilities:

Vulnerabilities are situations that are not considered in the program. For example, the simplest "weak password" vulnerability means that the system administrator forgot to block accounts in some network applications. The Perl program vulnerability may be due to the programmer's design. When the program considers the imperfect situation, the code segment that causes the program to be executed is overwhelmed. The overflow vulnerability belongs to the original design of the system or program, without pre-reserving sufficient resources, and in the future, the program is used. The resulting resources are insufficient; the special IP packet bomb is actually an error when the program analyzes some special data, etc...

Overall, the loophole is the human negligence in the design of the program, which cannot be absolutely avoided in any program; the hacker is using all kinds of loopholes to attack the network. The word "network security" at the beginning of this chapter is actually the meaning of "vulnerability". Hackers use vulnerabilities to complete various attacks is the ultimate result. In fact, the real definition of hackers is "the person looking for vulnerabilities." They are not cyber-attacks as fun, but are obsessed with reading other people's programs every day and trying to find the vulnerabilities. It should be said that, to a certain extent, hackers are "good people". They are committed to this line in pursuit of perfection and establishment of a secure Internet, but only because some hackers or simply hackers often exploit aggressive vulnerabilities. In recent years, people have been afraid of hackers and hostility.

6. Encryption and Decryption:

In the explanation of "Agreement", I mentioned "because of the problem of the grassroots of network design...", simply saying that this problem is to allow all Internet users to participate in information sharing, and thus for certain businesses, the transmission of personal privacy on the Internet will be exposed to the public. Others can access our credit cards, personal emails, etc. through monitoring or interception. How can we make this information safe? The reader may have thought of the "World War II" spy war as the participating countries used the telegram to encrypt the code. Only the receiver who knows the password can perform the decoding work. This ancient encryption method still has its vitality on the modern network. The information processed by encryption is transmitted on the network. No matter who gets the document, as long as there is no password, it is still in vain of.

The longest use on the network is to set a personal password, use DES encryption lock, these two encryption methods can complete the user login system, website, email mailbox and protection information package, and the work that hackers want to do is through the loophole. The brute force guessing, the reverse application of the encryption algorithm and other methods to obtain the plaintext of the encrypted file, some people use the "magic height one foot, the road high one" is used here, it is indeed appropriate! Encryption methods on the network and systems that require password verification are emerging, and hackers are looking for ways to crack these systems. It can be said that "vulnerabilities" and "decryption" are two completely different hacking fields. The preference of different learners for them will directly affect the types of hackers that will become in the future, so the choice between them It should be based on personal preferences and this book will focus on learning about the "vulnerabilities".

7. Trojan horse:

Trojan horse is a program; this program can be done by the programmer's intentional design. But the operation of the Trojan horse, whether or not the user understands it, is not endorsed. According to some people's knowledge, viruses are a special case of Trojan horses: they can be spread to other programs (that is, they are also turned into Trojan horses). According to another person's understanding, viruses that are not intentionally causing any damage are not Trojan horses. In the end, no matter how it is defined, many people only use "Trojan horses" to describe malicious programs that cannot be copied in order to distinguish Trojan horses from viruses.

Commonly Used Hacker Software Classifications

1. Prevention:

This is from A class of software involved in security perspectives, such as firewalls, virus checking software, system process monitors, port management programs, etc., belong to such software. This type of software maximizes the security and personal privacy of computer users and is not compromised by hackers. Network servers also attach great importance to the needs of such software. Log analysis software, system intrusion software, etc. can help administrators maintain servers and track hackers who invade the system.

2. Information collection:

Information collection software types, including port scanning, vulnerability scanning, weak password scanning and other scanning software; as well as monitoring, interception of information packets and other spyware software, most of which belong to the software is also true and evil.

That is to say, regardless of decent hackers, evil hackers, system administrators, or general computer users, user-like software can accomplish different purposes. In most cases, hacker-like software is more frequent because they rely on such software to scan the server in all directions, get as much information about the server as possible, and have a good understanding of the server. In order to carry out hacking.

3. Trojans and worms:

These are two types of software, but they work in much the same way, they are both virus-hidden and destructive, and people with control can also operate such software, or by prior Well-designed procedures do a certain amount of work. Of course, system administrators can also use this kind of software as a tool for remote management of servers.

4. Floods:

The so-called "flood", that is, information garbage bombs, can cause the target server to overload and crash through a large number of garbage requests. In recent years, DOS distributed attacks have become popular on the network. Simply put, it can also be classified as this. In the class software. Flood software can also be used as a mail bomb or chat bomb. These "fool" software has been streamlined and programmed by network security enthusiasts. Also, the software is often used in the hands of "pseudo-hackers" accused at the beginning of this book.

5. Password cracking:

The most practical way to ensure network security is to rely on the cryptosystem of various encryption algorithms. Hackers may be able to easily obtain a ciphertext password file, but if there is no encryption algorithm, it still cannot obtain the real password. Therefore, the use of password cracking software is imperative, using the computer's high-speed computing capabilities, such software can use password dictionary or exhaustive way to restore the encrypted essay.

6. Deception:

If you want to get the plaintext password mentioned above, the hacker needs to perform encryption algorithm restoration on the ciphertext, but if it is a complicated password, it is not so simple to crack. But is it more convenient to let the person who knows the password directly tell the prototype of the hacker password? Deception software is designed to accomplish this.

7. Camouflage:

The ISP and the server will record all kinds of operations on the network. If the hacker action is not performed after a good camouflage, it is easy to be traced to the hacker by the anti-tracking technology, so disguise its own IP. Address and identity are a very important part of the hacker's compulsory course, but camouflage technology requires deep knowledge of the network. This kind of software is used when there is no solid foundation at the beginning. The fourth important section you need to master is learning the basic environment of hackers.

First, the choice of operating system:

We often hear that hackers love Linux; this is because Linux provides a more flexible operation mode and more powerful functions than Windows. For example, for the forgery of IP addresses, it is easy to write special IP header information using Linux system, but it is almost impossible under Windows system. But Linux also has its shortcomings.

The commands in this system are complex and complicated, and are not suitable for beginners. For individual learners, not many people will give up "comfortable" Windows, give up wonderful computer games and convenient operation, go all out to hacker learning. And for beginner hackers, most of the network knowledge can be learned in the Windows system. Relative to the Linux system, the hacking software under the Windows platform is not infrequent. In addition, by installing the package, the Windows system can also be debugged. The amount of procedures, so the initial learning hacker does not have to start with Linux.

This book uses the platform kali Linux, because for individual users, NT or 2000 are somewhat more demanding - system configuration requirements are too high. However, the use of 95 or 98 lacks some of the necessary functions - NET, TELNET commands are not perfect. However, most of the contents of this book test vulnerabilities, starting from a remote server, so it is not necessary to learn kali Linux operating system.

Second, the commonly used software:

If your system is kali Linux, then tell you good news - you do not need to install too much extra software, because the hacking knowledge we contact depends on the commands and built-in software provided by the system can be done. In addition to the basic operating system, learners also need to install a variety of scanners, and then download a better Trojan software, a monitoring software, and there is no other demand. If necessary, readers can install the above software and learn its usage, but I want to tell you that for all kinds of bombs, as well as a variety of hacking software on the network, after learning this book, you can if you make your own and develop it yourself, there is no need to use software written by others.

For the scanner and monitoring software, I give the following suggestions, and the software will be described in detail later in the book: All three of these software's are free and powerful. Like Nmap and metasploit is a domestic software, he integrates a variety of scanning functions, and supports both console and graphical interface operations, as well as detailed vulnerability instructions. For beginners, with these two tools, learning hackers is more than enough.

Third, additional tools:

If you can install the following tools, it will be of great help to learn hackers, of course, the following software is mainly to learn additional content and for the "second part" learning to pave the way, so it hinders the study of this book.

1. Background server:

A background service program with some network applications can set up its own computer as a small server to learn the corresponding network application and understand its operation mechanism from internal. This will greatly improve its own the server's perceptual knowledge, while also being able to monitor the data on its own server when the server is activated and if there are other hackers to attack, you can clearly record the other party's attack process, and thus learn more hacking methods. For this book, we mainly introduce scripting language vulnerabilities such as Perl and ASP, so we can install an IIS or HTTPD. Then install Active Perl to make your own server have the ability to compile cgi and pl scripts. There is also a benefit to using your own server, which can save a lot of online time, and put the process of learning and finding vulnerabilities on your own computer, which saves money and poses no threat to the network.

2. C language compilation platform:

In future, when learning hackers, you will encounter many "problems of your own". These problems may not be noticed by others on the network, so you cannot find the corresponding program. At this time, learners It's a matter of developing the tools yourself, so installing a Borland C will be very convenient. Through this compiler, learners can learn both the C language and some of the small programs listed later in this book to create a self. Tool library.

3. The classification of network security software:

Now let's look at the classification of network security software, because learning hacker knowledge is two interrelated processes: learning how to be black, but also how to prevent hacking.

1. Firewall:

This is the most common security mechanism software on the network. The firewall has both hardware and software. Most readers may see software firewalls. Its functions are mainly to filter spam (to ensure that the system will not be bomb attacked), to prevent worm intrusion, to prevent hacking, to increase system privacy (protect sensitive data), to monitor system resources in real time, to prevent system crashes, and to maintain databases regularly. Backing up the main information... The firewall can fix the vulnerabilities in the system itself, so that the hacker has no chance to start. In addition, for enterprises with LANs, firewalls can limit the opening of system ports and prohibit certain network services (to prevent Trojans).

2. Detection software:

The Internet has a tool for clearing a hacker program, but this kind of software is more integrated in the anti-virus software or firewall software, for the Trojans and worms in the system can be detected and cleared, the software In order to protect the system from infringement, it will automatically protect the hard disk data, automatically maintain the registry file, detect the content of the code, and monitor the open status of the system port. If the user wants, the software can also write a script to shield the specified port (this function is the same as the firewall).

3. Backup tools:

Tools dedicated to backup data can help the server to regularly back up data, and update the data at the time of development, so that even if the hacker destroys the database on the server, the software can completely repair the received intrusion data in a short time. . In addition, for individual users, this kind of software can perform a full image backup of the hard disk. Once the system crashes, the user can restore the system to the original state by using such software. For example, Ghost is the leader in such software.

4. Log records, analysis tools:

For the server, the log file is essential, the administrator can use the log to understand the server's request type and request source, and according to the log to determine whether the system is hacked. Through log analysis software, administrators can easily anti-track intrusion hackers, find the source of hackers' attacks, and then catch hackers. This is why hackers use IP address masquerading, server hopping, and clearing log files after hacking the server.

Installing a Virtual Machine

People must be prepared for everything. Hackers are no exception. Before hackers invade other computers on the Internet, they need to do a series of preparations, including installing virtual machines on computers, preparing commonly used tools, and mastering common ones. Whether it is attack or training, hackers will not try to use a physical computer, but build a virtual environment in a physical computer, that is, install a virtual machine. In a virtual machine, hackers can intuitively perform various attack tests and complete most of the intrusion learning, including making viruses, Trojans, and implementing remote control.

A virtual machine is a computer system that is simulated by software, has a complete hardware system function, and runs in a completely isolated environment. The work that can be done on the physical machine can be implemented in the virtual machine. Because of this, more and more people are using virtual machines. When you create a new virtual machine on a computer, you need to use part of the hard disk and memory capacity of the physical machine as the hard disk and memory capacity of the virtual machine. Each virtual machine has its own CMOS, hard drive and operating system.

Users can partition and format the virtual machine, install operating system and application software, just like a physical machine. The Java Virtual Machine is an imaginary machine that is typically implemented by software simulation on a real computer. The Java virtual machine has its own imagined hardware, such as processors, stacks, registers, etc., and has a corresponding instruction system.

The Java virtual machine is mainly used to run programs edited by Java. Because the Java language has cross-platform features, the Java virtual machine can also directly run programs edited in Java language in multiple platforms without modification. The relationship between the Java virtual machine and Java is similar to the relationship between Flash Player and Flash.

There may be users who think that the virtual machine is just an analog computer, and at most, it can perform the same operations as a physical machine, so it does not have much practical significance. In fact, the biggest advantage of a virtual machine is virtualization. Even if the system in the virtual machine crashes or fails to run, it will not affect the operation of the physical machine. And it can also be used to test the latest version of the application or operating system, even if the installation of the application with the virus Trojan is no problem, because the virtual machine and the physical machine are completely isolated, the virtual machine will not leak in the physical machine data. VMware is a well-known and powerful virtual machine software that allows users to run two or more Windows and Linux systems simultaneously on the same physical machine.

Compared with the "multi-boot" system, VMware adopts a completely different concept. Multiple operating systems of a physical machine can only run one of the systems at the same time. The switching system needs to restart the computer, but VMware is different. It is the same. Multiple operating systems can be run at any time, thus avoiding the hassle of rebooting the system.

The VMware installer can be downloaded from some common resource offering sites such as filehippo.com. After downloading the VMware installer, you can extract and install it. After the installation is successful, the corresponding shortcut icon will be displayed on the desktop.

The following describes the steps to create a new virtual machine in VMware.

STEP01:

Start VMware Workstation by using the GUI interface.

STEP02:

Select a new virtual machine

STEP03:

Select the configuration type

STEP04:

Select to install the operating system later

STEP05:

Select the guest operating system

STEP06:

Set the virtual machine name and installation location

STEP07:

Specify virtual machine disk capacity

STEP08:

Click the "Finish" button.

Installation of Kali Linux

Nowadays, the installation process of Linux has been very "foolish", and the installation of the entire system can be completed with a few mouse clicks. The installation of the Kali Linux operating system is also very simple. This section describes the detailed process of installing Kali Linux to hard drive, USB drive. We will explain how to upgrade tools in the next section. Installing to a hard drive is one of the most basic operations. The implementation of this work allows users to run Kali Linux without using a DVD. Before you install this new operating system, you need to do some preparatory work. For example, where do you get Linux? What are the requirements for computer configuration? ... These requirements will be listed one by one below.

- The minimum disk space for Kali Linux installation is 8GB. For ease of use, it is recommended to save at least 25GB to save additional programs and files.

- The memory is preferably 512MB or more.

The official website provides 32-bit and 64-bit ISO files. This book uses 32-bit as an example to explain the installation and use. After downloading the ISO file, burn the image file to a DVD.

Then you can start to install Kali Linux to your hard drive.

1. Insert the installation CD into the CD-ROM of the user's computer, restart the system, and you will see the interface

2. This interface is the guiding interface of Kali, and the installation mode is selected on this interface. Selecting the Graphical Install here will display an interface.

3. Select the default language of the installation system in this interface is English, and then click the Continue button then the next interface will be shown.

4. In the interface selection area is "Your country", and then click the "Continue" button, the next interface will be displayed.

5. Select the keyboard mode as "English" in this interface, and then click "Continue" button, the next interface will be displayed.

6. This interface is used to set the host name of the system. Here, the default host name Kali is used (users can also

enter the name of their own system). Then click the "Continue" button, the next interface will be displayed.

7. This interface is used to set the domain name used by the computer. The domain name entered in this example is kali.example.com. If the current computer is not connected to the network, you can fill in the domain name and click the "Continue" button. The next interface will be displayed.

8. Set the root user password on this interface, and then click the "Continue" button, the next interface will be displayed.

9. This interface allows the user to select a partition. Select "Use the entire disk" here, and then click the "Continue" button, the next interface will be displayed.

10. This interface is used to select the disk to be partitioned. There is only one disk in the system, so the default disk is fine here. Then click the "Continue" button, the next interface will be displayed.

11. The interface requires a partitioning scheme, and three schemes are provided by default. Select "Place all files in the same partition (recommended for beginners)" and

click the "Continue" button, the next interface shown will be displayed.

12. Select "Partition setting ends and write the changes to disk" in the world, and then click "Continue" button, the next interface will be displayed. If you want to modify the partition, you can select "Undo the modification of the partition settings" in this interface to re-partition.

13. Select the "Yes" check box on this interface, and then click the "Continue" button, the next interface will be displayed.

14. Start installing the system now. Some information needs to be set during the installation process, such as setting up network mirroring. If the computer on which the Kali Linux system is installed is not connected to the network, select the "No" check box on this screen and click the "Continue" button. Select the "Yes" checkbox here and the next interface will be displayed.

15. Set the HTTP proxy information on this interface. If you do not need to connect to the external network through the HTTP proxy, just click the "Continue" button, the next interface will be displayed.

16. After the scanning mirror site is completed you can go to the next option

17. In the country where the image is selected, select "Your country" and click "Continue" button, the next interface will be displayed.

18. The interface provides 7 mirror sites by default, and one of them is selected as the mirror site of the system. Select mirrors.163.com here, then click the "Continue" button, the next interface will be displayed.

19. Select the "Yes" check box on this interface, and then click the "Continue" button, the next interface will be displayed. (20) The installation will continue at this time. After the installation, process is finished kali Linux login screen will appear.

Installing kali Linux using a USB drive

The Kali Linux USB drive provides the ability to permanently save system settings, permanently update and install packages on USB devices, and allows users to run their own personalized Kali Linux.

Create a bootable Live USB drive for the Linux distribution on the Win32 Disk Imager, which includes continuous storage for Kali Linux. This section describes the steps to install Kali Linux to a USB drive. Installing an operating system onto a USB drive is a bit different from installing to a hard drive. So, you need to do some preparation before installing.

For example, where do you get Linux? USB drive format? What is the size of the USB drive? These requirements will be listed one by one below. After the previous preparations are completed, you can install the system.

The steps to install Kali Linux onto a USB drive are as follows.

1. Insert a formatted and writable USB drive into the Windows system. After inserting, the display next interface is shown.

2. Start Win32 Disk Imager, the startup interface is shown. In the Image File location, click the icon to select the location of the Kali Linux DVD ISO image and select the USB device where Kali Linux will be installed. The device in this example is K. After selecting the ISO image file and USB device, click the Write button to write the ISO file to the USB drive.

3. Use the UNetbootin tool to make the device K a USB boot disk. Launch the UNetbootin tool and the next interface will be displayed.

4. Select the "Disc Image" checkbox in this interface, then select the location of the ISO file and set the Space used to preserve files across reboots to 4096MB.

5. Select the USB drive, the USB drive in this example is K, and then click the "OK" button; it will start to create a bootable USB drive.

6. After the creation is completed, the next interface will be displayed.

7. At this point, the USB drive is created successfully. In the interface, click the "Restart Now" button, enter the BIOS boot menu and select USB boot, you can install the Kali Linux operating system. When users use it for a while, they may be dissatisfied with working in a system that does not change at all, but are eager to upgrade their Linux as they would on a Windows system.

In addition, Linux itself is an open system, new software appears every day, and Linux distributions and kernels are constantly updated. Under such circumstances, it is very urgent to learn to upgrade Linux. This section will introduce Kali updates and upgrades.

Updating and Upgrading kali Linux

The specific steps for updating and upgrading Kali are as follows.

1. Select "Application" | "System Tools" | "Software Update" command in the graphical interface, and the next interface will be displayed.

2. The interface prompts to confirm whether the application should be run as a privileged user. If you continue, click the "Confirm Continue" button, the next interface will be displayed.

3. The interface shows that a total of packages need to be updated. Click the "Install Update" button to display the interface.

4. This interface shows the packages that the update package depends on. Click the "Continue" button to display the interface.

5. From this interface you can see a progress of the software update. In this interface, you can see a different status of each package. Among them, the package

appears behind the icon, indicating that the package is downloading; if displayed as icons indicate the package has been downloaded; if there is at the same time and icon, then, that after you install this package, you need to reboot the system; these packages installed once successful, it will appear as an icon. At this point, click the "Exit" button and restart the system. During the update process, downloaded packages will automatically jump to the first column. At this point, scrolling the mouse is useless.

6. After restarting the system, log in to the system and execute the lsb_release -a command to view all version information of the current operating system.

7. From the output information, you can see that the current system version is 2.2.1. The above commands apply to all Linux distributions, including RedHat, SuSE, and Debian. If you only want to view the version number, you can view the /etc/issue file. Execute the command as follows: root@kali:~#cat/etc/issueKali GNU/Linux 2.2.1\n\1

A Hacking Roadmap

If a hacker wants to attack a target computer, it can't be done by DOS commands. It also needs some powerful intrusion tools, such as port scanning tools, network sniffing tools, Trojan making tools, and remote-control tools.

This section will briefly introduce the intrusion tools commonly used by hackers.

a) Port scanning

The port scanning tool has the function of scanning the port. The so-called port scanning means that the hacker can scan the information of the target computer by sending a set of port scanning information. These ports are intrusion channels for the hacker. Once the hacker understands these ports, the hacker can invade the target computer. In addition to the ability to scan the open ports of a computer, the port scan tool also has the ability to automatically detect remote or target computer security vulnerabilities. Using the port scan tool, users can discover the distribution of various TCP ports on the target computer without leaving traces. And the services provided to allow users to indirectly or directly understand the security issues of the target computer. The port scanning tools commonly used by hackers are SuperScan and X-Scan.

b) Sniffing tool

A sniffing tool is a tool that can sniff packets on a LAN. The so-called sniffing is to eavesdrop on all the packets flowing through the LAN. By eavesdropping and analyzing these packets, you can peek at the private information of others on the LAN. The sniffing tool can only be used in the local area network, and it is impossible to directly sniff the target computer on the Internet. The data sniffing tools commonly used by hackers are Sniffer Pro and Eiffel Web Detective.

c) Trojan making

tool As the name suggests, Trojan making tools are tools for making Trojans. Since Trojans have the function of stealing personal privacy information of the target computer, many junior hackers like to use Trojans to make Trojans directly. The Trojan creation tool works basically the same way. First, the tool is used to configure the Trojan server program. Once the target computer runs the Trojan server program, the hacker can use the Trojan tool to completely control the target computer of the Trojan.

The operation of the Trojan making tool is very simple, and the working principle is basically the same, so many junior hackers favor it. Trojan horse making tools commonly used by hackers are "glacial" Trojans and bundled Trojans.

d) Remote control tools

Remote control tools are tools with remote control functions that can remotely control the target computer, although the control methods are different (some remote-control tools are remotely controlled by implanting a server program, and some remote-control tools are used to directly control the LAN).

All computers in the middle), but once the hacker uses the remote-control tool to control the target computer, the hacker acts as if it were sitting in front of the target computer. The remote-control tools commonly used by hackers are network law enforcement officers and remote control.

Hacking Target Computers

In Internet, in order to prevent hackers from invading their own computers, it is necessary to understand the common methods of hacking target computers. The intrusion methods commonly used by hackers include data-driven attacks, illegal use of system files, forged information attacks, and remote manipulation. The following describes these intrusion methods.

1) *A data driven attack*

A data-driven attack is an attack initiated by a hacker who sends or copies a seemingly harmless special program to a target computer. This attack allows hackers to modify files related to network security on the target computer, making it easier for hackers to invade the target computer the next time. Data-driven attacks mainly include buffer overflow attacks, format string attacks, input verification attacks, synchronous vulnerability attacks, and trust vulnerability attacks.

2) *Forgery information attack*

Forgery information attack means that the hacker constructs a fake path between the source computer and the target computer by sending the forged routing information, so that the data packets flowing to the target computer are all passed through the computer operated by the hacker, thereby obtaining the bank account in the data packet. Personal sensitive information such as passwords.

3) Information protocol

In a local area network, the source path option of the IP address allows the IP packet to choose a path to the target computer itself. When a hacker attempts to connect to an unreachable computer A behind a firewall, he only needs to set the IP address source path option in the sent request message so that one of the destinations addresses of the packet points to the firewall, but the final address points to Computer A. The message is allowed to pass when it reaches the firewall because it points to the firewall instead of computer A. The IP layer of the firewall processes the source path of the packet and sends it to the internal network. The message arrives at the unreachable computer A, thus achieving a vulnerability attack against the information protocol.

4) Remote operation

Remote operation means that the hacker launches an executable program on the target computer. The program will display a fake login interface. When the user enters the login information such as account and password in the interface, the program will input the account and password. Transferred to the hacker's computer. At the same time, the program closes the login interface and prompts the "system failure" message, asking the user to log in again. This type of attack is similar to a phishing website that is often encountered on the Internet.

5) LAN security

In the local area network, people are one of the most important factors of LAN security. When the system administrator has a mistake in the configuration of the WWW server system and the user's permission to expand the user's authority, these mistakes can provide opportunities for the hacker. Hackers use these mistakes, plus the command of finger, netstat, etc., to achieve intrusion attacks. Resending an attack means that the hacker collects specific IP data packets and tampers with the data, and then resends the IP data packets one by one to spoof the target computer receiving the data to implement the attack. In the LAN, the redirect message can change the router's routing list. Based on these messages, the router can suggest that the computer take another better path to propagate the data. The ICMP packet attack means that the hacker can effectively use the redirect message to redirect the connection to an unreliable computer or path, or to forward all the packets through an unreliable computer.

6) Vulnerability attack

A vulnerability attack for source path selection means that the hacker transmits a source path message with an internal computer address to the local area network by operating a computer located outside the local area network. Since the router will trust this message, it will send an answer message to the computer located outside the LAN, as this is the source path option requirement for IP. The defense against this type of attack is to properly configure the router to let the router discard packets that are sent from outside the LAN but claim to be from internal computers.

7) Ethernet broadcast attack

The Ethernet broadcast attack mode refers to setting the computer network card interface to promiscuous, to intercept all the data packets in the local area network, analyze the account and password saved in the data packet, and steal information.

UNIX

On the Internet, servers or supercomputers on many websites use the UNIX operating system. The hacker will try to log in to one of the computers with UNIX, get the system privilege through the vulnerability of the operating system, and then use this as a base to access and invade the rest of the computer. This is called Island-hopping.

A hacker often jumps a few times before attacking the final destination computer. For example, a hacker in the United States may log in to a computer in Asia before entering the FBI network, then log in to a computer in Canada, then jump to Europe, and finally from France. The computer launched an attack on the FBI network. In this way, even if the attacked computer finds out where the hacker launched the attack, it is difficult for the administrator to find the hacker. What's more, once a hacker gains the system privileges of a computer, he can delete the system log when exiting and cut "vine".

In almost all protocol families implemented by UNIX, a well-known vulnerability makes it possible to steal TCP connections. When a TCP connection is being established, the server acknowledges the user request with a response message containing the initial sequence number. This serial number has no special requirements, as long as it is unique.

After the client receives the answer, it will confirm it once and the connection will be established.

The TCP protocol specification requires a serial number of 250,000 replacements per second. The actual replacement frequency of most UNIX systems is much smaller than this number, and the number of next replacements is often predictable, and hackers have this predictable server initial. The ability of the serial number allows the intrusion attack to be completed. The only way to prevent this attack is to make the initial sequence number more random.

The safest solution is to use the encryption algorithm to generate the initial sequence number. The resulting extra CPU load is now the hardware speed. It can be ignored.

On UNIX systems, too many files can only be created by superusers, and rarely by a certain type of user. This makes it necessary for system administrators to operate under root privileges. This is not very safe. Since the primary target of hacking is root, the most frequently attacked target is the superuser's password. Strictly speaking, the user password under UNIX is not encrypted.

It is just a key for encrypting a common string as a DES algorithm. There are now a number of software tools for decryption that use the high speed of the CPU to search for passwords. Once the attack is successful, the hacker becomes an administrator on the UNIX system.

Therefore, the user rights in the system should be divided, such as setting the mail system administrator management, and then the mail system mail administrator can manage the mail system well without superuser privileges, which makes the system much safer.

CHAPTER 2:

BASH AND PYTHON SCRIPTING

This chapter will give a good introduction to bash a command line interface language and python a famous programming language. By learning bash and python as a hacker, you can increase your skills exponentially. You may feel overwhelmed looking at all of the code that you might have never seen before.

Try to practice code by doing small little projects and automate tasks with python you will become an experienced hacker in very short time. Different sections in the chapter will help you understand things easily and will let you learn scripting effectively.

Let's start!

What is a shell?

In windows systems we have a GUI that helps us to run programs. Of Course, Linux based systems also consists of a GUI. But apart from GUI Linux based systems consist of a powerful interface called shell a command line interface. Basically, shell helps the users to run a program or software using a command prompt. Shell can be executed directly using commands or by a file called as shell scripts that can be easily created by a text editor or an IDE.

What is UNIX?

UNIX is an operating system that Linux and many operating systems are based upon. Learning about UNIX history can help us learn about the importance of shell in programming world.

What is the bash?

There are many types of shell types. Among them Bash is one of the most familiar UNIX shell that is simple and can be used to automate many tasks in the system.

What is a terminal?

Terminal is just like a browser for websites. It is developed for the client and for his comfort. People use terminals to type commands and start shell processing. Every operating system has a command terminal. For example, even windows have a terminal called MS-DOS, which has a lot of difference from the Linux terminals.

Looking at a terminal

Linux terminals are very easy to understand. When starting the terminal is an user in kali Linux we can see "userofthesystem@machinename" format followed by a $.

Before going to learn about the bash in detail, we will just go through few examples that will explain how bash works.

1) echo

You might have already heard it many times. This just displays whatever written inside it as the output.

$echo ' That's a good bash terminal'

output: That's a good bash terminal

2) date

This bash command displays the present date and time as output.

This is used very commonly while doing scripting.

$date

Output: Sun Dec 20 23:32:12 PST 2019

3) *Calendar*

$cal

This will just display the calendar of the month that you are in. We will give a simple example by creating a shell file instead of directly executing in the command.

This process is explained below in detail.

Step 1:

In the first step open, a text editor you wish and create a file named example.sh and start writing the following lines.

!/bin/bash

echo " This happens in every shell" // This prints as output

We will explain the shell program line by line now. The first line will just order the file to open in a bash shell. And the second line as we already discussed will print the text in between quotes as output. The next to it is a comment that can be written for the help of reader or programmer.

Step 2:

Save the file.

In the next immediate step to execute the following shell script file, we need to modify the permission of it.

This can be done using the following command.

chmod +x example.sh // This will create a executable permission to the script

Step 3:

In the last step, we need to execute the file in the command to get an output.

We can use following commands to get an output.

$ bash example.sh

$ ./example.sh

Output:

This happens in every shell We can use the command Clear to clear everything on the shell.

$ clear

In the next section, we will explain some basic bash commands that are available in kali Linux.

These are very important to learn for a better understanding of the Linux system functions.

1) pwd

This command will print the present working directory that the user is in. You can even look as a tree directory with additional options.

$ pwd

Output: /user/rod

2) ls

This command will show the present directory contents that is all of its files and folders. We normally use it to look at the present directory files.

$ ls

Output:

shell.py shell.img shell.png

3) cd

This command is used to change the directory. Get ready with the path that you want to navigate to and add cd before it. You can check whether the directory is changed or not by using ls command.

$ cd /home/desktop/

4) mkdir

This command can be used to make a new directory or new folder.

$ mkdir new/ruby

5) mv

This command helps us to move files or folders from one directory to other. It follows the following pattern.

$ mv sourcepath destinationpath

for example:

$ mv plus.py plus/code

6) touch

This is a special command that can be used to create a new file of any type in a director. For example, let's create an empty text file called example.py in the present directory.

$ touch example.txt

7) rm

This command helps us to remove a file from the disk. This will completely delete the file. So use with a caution.

$ rm example.txt

8) rmdir

This command removes the directory from the disk.

rmdir python/pythonfiles

9) cat

This command can be used to read the text file and display everything present on in the output screen.

$ cat rowdy.txt

Output:

Apple

Bat

Car

Dog . . .

This will display everything that is present in the rowdy.txt text file. However, when trying to display a txt file with large number of data it can become quite clumsy. So, to get rid of this we use the below command.

10) less

This command displays the huge chunk of data in one page per time. This will help us by using certain gestures. Spacebar can take us to next page whereas b will take us to the previous page.

$ less rowdy.txt

In the next section, we will describe about important concepts called pipelines and filters that can be used for organization and other purposes.

1) Pipelines

This explicitly means to give output of the first command as an input to second command.

command1 | command2

Where | is called as a pipe operator.

2) Filters

Filters are an extra technique used to separate or organize a data. Linux and bash consist of many filter commands to find and organize data.

a) grep This command helps to find a word in a text file easily. The command is as follows to understand about the functionality of grep command.

$ grep raj cricket.txt

This will display everything that matches raj in the text file.

b) sort This command will help to sort the contents in the file alphabetically or numerically.

Example for pipelines & filters:

$cat animals.txt | sort // $ command textfile pipeline(|) filter

Output:

Cat

Dog

Monkey

Zebra

Now we have mastered all the basic bash properties and now will dive into more complex topics that will explain the bash in depth.

1) Variables

Variables are an important piece of memory that stores the data given as input or while executing. The data to be processed should contain variables that have different data types. In short, variable is like an address box and can be modified or replaced with another variable if given correct instructions. Bash also consists of variables and can be used to write command line instructions that can-do various tasks. Bash variables are quite different from other variables because they are of two types. Below we will explain about them in detail.

1. System variables

These variables are pre created by Linux and can be used while scripting to fill a particular value.

These are represented by capital letters.

Example:

USERNAME ----> This variable defines the current logged in user name. You can call it to get the specific output.

2. User variables

These are variables which are the user generated and can be used for complex tasks. Lower case letters represent these. In bash, variables can store any data irrespective of datatype we normally use in programming languages.

a) Define a variable

Here is the syntax

$ room = bad

b) To use a variable

$room

c) Now you can use this command to print the following variable using echo command.

echo $room

Output:

Bad

d) We can also use this variable in a string for printing it.

This is quite easy and a very useful function.

$ echo " This is $room"

output:

This is bad

Conditionals in the Bash

This is a normal if and else statement that is used in programming languages. We will explain this with an example below.

This is a bash script to describe conditioning

if [15 -lt 25]

then

echo " This is smaller"

if

output :

This is smaller

In the above example we just explained about an if statement and in the next example we will use an example with an else statement too.

This explains both if and else

if [35 -lt 25]

then

echo "This is the biggest number"

else

echo "This is the lesser number"

if

Output:

This is the biggest number

Looping in shell script:

Looping means to repeat the same thing with a definite interval. Bash has for lop and while loop. To understand this precisely we will use this following example.

bash program for for loop

for j in 6 7 8 9

do

echo "This is $j"

done

Output :

This is 6

This is 7

This is 8

This is 9

Functions in shell script:

Function is a set of instructions that need to be followed in a definite way. Bash provides many inbuilt functions and we can also create user made functions as shown below.

syntax to create a function addition

()

{

echo ' Sum is $a + $b'

return }

Now we need to call that function addition

Output:

If variables are 2 and 3, we will get output as

Sum is 5

This ends our journey to the world of shell scripting. There are many more bash scripting patterns and commands that you need to master to be a proficient hacker.

What is scripting?

Scripting is just programming but used in terms when programming is done in small code and used specifically to do a task rather than developing software with all modules combined.

Many programming languages can be learnt easily in now a days. But python is considered the best for beginners due to its huge resources and modules and open source content that will help beginners to master the scripting easily and effectively.

Why hackers need to learn scripting?

This is a very basic question to deal with beginners because they might have seen few tutorials about an application that can do everything and is termed as hacking by the novice author. People who do things with the help of software's developed by other hackers are called as script kiddies in hacking terms.

Always remember that to be a professional hacker you need to create small scripting codes that can automate things and can-do tasks effectively unlike normal people. Also scripting can help you understand things better and can create an overview of all the technologies that are being used. Inclining to a programming language is not a problem but hackers need to learn a lot of programming languages to understand the syntax. In the next section, we will describe about python programming in detail with examples.

Why python is superior?

Python is considered by hackers due to its enormous third party modules that can be installed using pip command. All these modules and one source scripts can help a beginner hacker to understanding how things work. And also python supports both functional and object oriented language making python a best bet for not only hackers but also everyone who are trying to learn programming.

First of all, you need an IDE or text editor to write your scripts on. There are numerous python IDE's in kali Linux. But we will first create a file named example.py and edit it using leafpad for executing it in the terminal. Pycharm by JetBrains is considered as the best python IDE in the market right now. Now we will discuss in detail about different concepts in python for getting started with it.

1) Variables

Variables are memory blocks that can be designated in a way that they can be invoked by any data type. There are different types of data type like int, float, string, list, tuples and dictionaries. All these try to store a value in their designated memory. Variables are implemented by the assignment operator and are called using their name.

this = " reddy"

print (Hi + this)

Output:

Hi reddy

Save the above code in a file called as pythontest.py and try to execute t from the command terminal.

First, you will need to give executive permissions to the python file using the following command.

root @ kali : chmod 755 example.py

This gets executive permission and need to be executed using the following command.

root@kali : ./example.py

Below we explain with different examples about different application of variables as shown below.

a) String

   this = " How to get it fast"

b) Integer

   this = 12

c) floating point variable

   this = 3.1222

d) List

   this = [2,3,45,23]

e) Dictionary

   this = { 'how' : is , 'this' : red}

Comments

Comments are something that doesn't goes with the program but is made for the convenience of programmers and users. You can just use text between three quotes to make a comment.

''' This is a comment '''

Functions:

Functions are the special programs that are used in a program. They usually make a program and repeat them altogether in many programs or many times in the same programs. Functions can be called in many times as needed.

help() is a function in kali Linux. In fact, many prebuilt functions are trying to make the user experience more comfortable.

Lists & Dictionaries:

We will talk in detail about lists and dictionaries in detail because they are special datatypes and can be used to accommodate more data and more techniques. It is normally referred as arrays that can be added subtracted and removed when t deals with the number of elements.

a) For example, our list example is

example = [1,2,3,4,5,6]

We can use example[2] to get the output as 3. And if use example [3]= 8 the list changes automatically. Here is the code below.

example[4] = 8

print example[]

output:

1,2,3,4,8,6

Modules:

Modules are exceptional python files that can be used again and again in python files. You can make your own scanning strategy as a python module and can call it whenever you reboot with system. This is one of the practical implementation of modules.

import metasploit

This is how we use Modules in python

If -conditionals in python:

Conditional statement is one of the most important python techniques that needs to be mastered because it decreases a lot of code and helps us decide something between two things. This simple conditional statement blocks will help us create much more complex scripting.

Example:

if this==0

print (" hurray")

else

print (" Didnt happen')

Looping statements:

Ever wondered how you get the same place in computer games? This is due to the looping function that programs implement. Basically looping means to repeat the same thing in an interval. Looping statements are complex and can be used to make wonders.

1) While loop

```
// A program to understand while loop
this = 3
while ( this <=7):
print ( this)
this + = 1
```

While loop simply while starting to loopback will check a boolean expression and if it is true it will take a loop and if it is false it will stop the loop.

2) For loop

For loop works differently when compared to while loop. This will let us use every variable that is available in our variable set until it satisfies the condition. For loop is like a brute force tool with conditions.

// Example for loop

for username in usernames:

result = connect (usr,pwd)

if

result == " Tom"

print (username + "found")

output:

Tom found

Object oriented programming:

Although being a modular and function-oriented language python also adopted object-oriented methodology that helped to create hundreds of software due to its flexibility and modularity. We will explain about different concepts of object-oriented programming in detail here.

What is a class?

Class is a model or strategy that organizes everything at a one place. Every method and variable that can be used are organized and called as a class.

What is an object?

This is where the actual work is done. This makes methods or connections with every variable or instance to get a desired result that you wish for.

What is a superclass?

Instead of all over creating the methods, again python uses inheritance to use other classes methods by a method called inheritance. Exception Handling While writing scripts we often encounter errors and bugs. This can be eliminated before or can be used to show warning using try, catch and try block. Learn about this before starting experimenting with scripting.

CHAPTER 3:
BASIC KALI LINUX CONCEPTS

Analyzing and managing networks

Hackers always tend to do quite complex things that can be tracked easily by forensic investigation. All major companies try to deploy forensic specialists and security investigators to find the details about the attacker after an attack.

This says that being a hacker is not easy and one who aspires to be a hacker need to know a lot about networking and its management like spoofing his ip or physical mac address.

This section will help us to learn in detail about these techniques in kali Linux for a better attack probability.

ifconfig

This is a basic network command that is used in all Linux distributions to check the connected networks with the computer.

You can find both wired and wireless connections using this command. To use this command, you need to have root privileges as it contacts with the kernel to get more information about the network devices that are connected.

Command is below:

root@kali : ifconfig

after clicking the above command, you will get an output that displays the network devices that are connected.

If there are Ethernet based connection that is wired they will be represented as eth followed by a subscript of a number that starts from 0 like eth0, eth1, eth2 and so on. You will also find MAC and Ip address of the particular network. We can use this information while doing an attack for making things difficult to find. Ifconfig also displays wlan0 that is about a wireless adapter that is within your system. "Hwaddr " also called as MAC address is displayed and this can be widely used in aircrack-ng while you are trying to attack a WIFI access point. The next section will describe about how to know about wireless connections in detail.

iwconfig

In your kali Linux terminal as a root user, click the following command to know more about wireless interfaces that are connected to the system.

root @ kali : iwconfig

This will display about the wireless connection along with its encryption like WPA, WEP and its physical address. For any hacker who is trying to capture packets for gaining sensitive information a good overview about wireless adapter can make the process more interesting.

How to change ip address?

A very basic idea that everyone knows is every network connection is distinguished by an address called as an IP address. It is easy to track down the information if someone obtains your network address. And for hackers who always try to attack hosts this would be a problem. But don't worry because there are few techniques and tricks, which you can use to spoof your address while doing a password attack or DOS attack.

Below section will help you get more information about this process. process to spoof ip address:

Step 1:

First of all, try to find the current ip address of the wired or wireless connection you are wishing to spoof using ifconfig or iwconfig command. Let us assume that the Ip address of our current wireless connection wlan0 is 192.232.2.1

Step 2:

Now use the following command for example to wlan0 i.e a wireless network to change the IP address.

root @ kali: ifconfig wlan0 192.112.3.2

Now when you click enter the ip address is spoofed in the background and all your processes from now on will use this spoofed ip address for attacking.

Step 3:

If you want to check if everything has been gone right use the same command ifconfig or iwconfig and you will observe the spoofed ip address as the network address.

Application:

Hackers can use this to make password attacks using john the ripper or THC hydra tools without being blocked by the network administrator. We can use advanced methodologies that can randomly spoof IP addresses in a certain interval of time for intrusion detection systems failing to detect the attack that is going on.

How to spoof your MAC address?

Just like how every network connection has an address the device that is connected to the network has a physical address called as MAC address. For example, an Android phone or IOS phone will have a MAC address just like a computer or Laptop. Manufacturers use different international organized rules to give MAC addresses.

Why MAC address spoofing should be done?

When you are hacking every trace of you should be spoofed especially your physical device information. Your network provider or Government can easily obtain information about you with a single click. Moreover spoofing MAC address can help you attack the same target many times. Script kiddies use certain applications to do this automatically. We will learn how to do this in kali Linux in the next section.

Step 1:

First of all, you can't change physical address when it is functioning. So, you need to down the network interface first. To down a network interface in kali Linux use the following command.

root @ kali: ifconfig eth2 down

Step 2:

Now you can change MAC address using two options. If you are trying to change MAC address for an Ethernet use the keyword ether and if it is a physical device like A mobile or Laptop use hw along with the new spoofed MAC address you wish to replace it with. Below is the command.

For Ethernet:

root @ kali: ifconfig ether A2:D3:T6:Z5:K9

For hardware devices:

root @ kali: ifconfg hw W2:E3:Y7:U8:I9

Step 3:

After using the above command, the MAC address changes and you need to up the network to make it work as like before.

The command is as follows:

root @ kali: ifconfig eth2 up

Manipulating Domain Name Service system in kali Linux

What is DNS?

Domain name service system is like a phone book for domain names. It will be very difficult to enter ip address if we want to access a website. So people have developed a system that will let us point out to an ip address when we enter a domain. When we click enter in browser URL the request will first go to DNS and it will verify whether the URL is available or not and gives its IP address if true.

dig command

This will just display the ip address to the URL we says. This will just look at the name server system and gives us results.

An example is given below.

root @ kali : dig bing.com

Output:

bing.com IN

yahoodns.net yahoodns.net 182.232.22.1

Can we change our domain server?

This can be easily done using the configuration file. Head on to the configuration file and open it using leafpad or your favorite text editor.

When you open /etc/resolv.conf you will find a line called

nameserver '192.234.2.1'

You can replace this with google DNS server for better security.

Can we change hosts file?

Host files consists of IP addresses that a particular software can use. You can stop or start firewalls using host files.

Just head on to /etc/hosts.conf and edit it according to your needs. Hackers use this commonly to stop updates to a cracked software or application.

File and directory permissions

Hackers' common targets are multinational companies where there are a lot of employees working around the corner day and night. If every directory and file can be accessed by everyone in the organization hackers' job would become very easy to use social engineering techniques to get access to the organizational files and directories. Also, explicit permissions can help network administrators to organize everything easily without giving a pathway people with malicious intent trying to execute dangerous files in the network.

Why this matter to Hackers?

Now a day's security is a mainstream issue and everyone are maintaining standards and doing security checks to not be attacked. However, if a hacker finds a backdoor to enter into the system, he needs to modify users and directory permissions first to get full access into the system. For this reason, budding hackers should not have a good overview on type of users and all directory permissions that Linux offers.

Types of Users

This is quite simple to understand and easy to implement if you are a network administrator. We will have a root user and other users in groups for better organization. We will explain this is detail in the following section.

a) Root user:

Root user is the one who have a complete privilege to access the network. If a hacker enters into a system network, he would always try to get root privileges for the functionality it offers. Basically, a root user can maintain everyone else in the network and can execute scripts or programs that can change how a network function.

b) Group users:

Imagine a simple scenario where there is an organization that has different departments like programming, debugging, testing and marketing. We need to create

Process management

Linux or any other typical operating system has many services and processes that run-in background and foreground. For example, in windows you can use taskbar to check the processes that are going on simultaneously. Whereas in Linux it becomes quite complex to check and kill processes that are eating more system power and memory.

What is a process?

Process is something that every operating system uses to maintain a lot of software's and applications that operates in background and foreground. For example, if you are using an antivirus it uses different set of processes to monitor everything that goes on in the system.

Why does it matter to hackers?

Imagine attacking a system and gaining access into it. What is the first thing you need to do? Obviously, you need to disable or kill all intrusion detection systems, Antivirus and Firewall to make things difficult for investigators to find you. To kill processes, you need to master few commands in Linux to view and disable or kill them. A good hacker will use certain strategies or techniques to find alarming processes that may alert the administrator and kill them as soon as possible. Below section describes different strategies that you need to use

How to view processes?

If you want to processes running on the Linux system you just need to enter a simple command called ps.

Just go to the Linux Terminal as a root user and enter as below.

root @ kali : ps

When you click the above command, you will get an output that looks bizarre for beginners. But we will review it so that you can understand it better.

Output:

PID	TTY	TIME	CMD
23435	pts/0	00:00:01	bash

If you observe it you will notice that this is simple and is not letting, you know about any process that are being run in the system.

So to get away with this confusion just add aux after the ps command in the terminal and now look at the output.

root @ kali : ps aux

Now you will get a lot of processes that are going on background and foreground. If you are running the command with Root privileges, you will see every process that is going on and if you run with user privilege then you will see processes that are running on your user system. We will just look at the output to discuss more about the keywords mentioned there.

Output:

USER PID %CPU %MEM VSZ RSS TTY

START TIME COMMAND

ROOT 23232 12.2 8.6 3423 32434 ?

12:34 00:32 /chrome

Here you can observe the output and can define the following terms

1. USER - This explains about the type of user that the process is being used

2. PID - This just gives an ID for the process

3. % CPU - Will let you know about the power of CPU that is being consumed by the particular process

4. % MEM - Will let you know about the Memory of CPU that is being consumed by the particular process

5. START - Will let you know about the starting time of the particular process

6. TIME - Will let you know about the number of seconds/minutes that the process is being alive

7. COMMAND - Will let you know by which the process has been started (More like a path of the origin)

By using these terms, you can find the processes and analyze them when you have access to a target system. In the next section, we will know how to filter processes.

Filtering by process name

When you use the command said before you will be bombarded with so many processes that has been running on the Linux. It will be overwhelming for a beginner to find the essential process by manual searching.

Here we will know about grep command to find the desired process with an example.

Step 1:

To understand this method let us use Nmap as an example. Nmap is a famous kali Linux tool that can be used for part scanning and information gathering. Login as a root user and call Nmap using the below command.

root @ kali : nmap

You can understand that the process has started by seeing the opening message by Nmap.

Step 2:

When the process starts just open a new terminal and enter the following command to find the processes initiated by Nmap easily

root @ kali > ps aux | grep nmap

Now you will get an output that displays every process that is directly involved with Nmap. By using grep command, you can easily find the processes instead of manual searching. That's what hackers do. Simplifying things and being smart.

Find most power and memory consuming processes

This is a trick that experienced hackers use to find the most important processes. Always remember the fact that processes that consume more memory and power are running in background all the time and monitoring the system. To find the most greeting process use the following command.

root @ kali:

top when you click the word top in the Linux terminal, you will get a result that highlights the most power and memory consuming process. In the next section, we will learn about prioritizing and killing processes with various commands.

Why processes need to be prioritized?

As a hacker, you need to multitask various things in order to be productive and crack the target as soon as possible. While doing this you may need to open many programs and software's and make everything messy. Prioritization is important because it lets you decide which more important task is. If you find that, the process is not necessary you can just kill the process. We will learn about this in detail.

nice command

It is one of the easiest methods to prioritize the processes and increase or decrease their priority by a certain range. This range varies from -19 to +19 where 0 is the default priority.

For suppose let us assume that there is a process named kaliprocess in desktop. We need to decrease its priority and allot it to other resources. To do that effectively we can use the following command.

root @ kali: nice -n 5 /desktop/kaliprocess

We can also use it to increase priority by giving -5 to the priority. We will use the same kaliprocess in desktop to demonstrate this. Here is the command.

root @ kal : nice -n -5 /desktop/kaliprocess

This will make the system to allocate more resources and increase its priority. renice command renice also does the same priority based processing but by using a different way. Using nice we used a margin to increase or decrease the priority, but by using renice we can give a certain priority value along with process id to make it happen. We will see it in a command example below.

root @ kali : renice 12 23221

How to kill a process?

When we are using a Linux based system as a hacker after successfully hacking the system, we need to kill processes for our safety. We also need to start using it when we are using more number of utilities to not get freezed in the desktop. Below we will learn about in detail.

root @ kali : kill -signal pid

Above command is the way to kill a process where signal stands for particular commands or rules that can be used and pid stands for processid. More than 50 kill signals can be used to kill a process in different ways. We will explain some of them below with examples. This is a very essential skill a hacker needs to develop. Few kill signals are explained here below with examples:

1. SIGQUIT

The kill signal option is 3. It will kill the process but all the data will be stored in a corememory and can be saved into a directory before quitting itself.

kill -3 3345

2. SIGHUP

The kill signal is 1. Here the process gets killed and is again restarted with the same pid.

kill -1 2324

3. SIGKILL

The kill signal is 9. This is very efficient process to kill the processes forever. This will make everything shut indefinitely and cannot be achieved again. Use with caution.

CHAPTER 4:
ADVANCED KALI LINUX CONCEPTS

Using abusive services

Services are the most important mechanisms that Linux operates for a better functioning of the operating system. Even windows have services that run-in background.

Basically, services are processes that run in the background until you use it. For example, consider a proxy server like Burp suite that will intercept every information that goes on in the browser and if you click No it stops the service and nothing goes there. In windows, which is quite well dominated by graphical user, interfaces services are easily closed down by a click. Whereas in Linux we need to start using command line to start, stop and restart services.

Why services matter to hackers?

Hackers should be well learnt about services because when you are trying to exploit a system you need to stop services that can interrupt what you are doing. Clever administrators use services to make hackers confuse. So, you need to understand the services that are making your exploitation difficult and stop them as soon as possible. Some advanced hackers install their own services after exploiting the system in a way that they will receive valuable information from the host regularly. In the below section we will explain with command line examples that will help us understand dealing with services.

We will explain this with an example using Burp suite service. Burp suite a java-based proxy interception service that can help web penetration testers find flaws in the websites. We will explain about this in detail in our next chapters. But for now, we will learn about how to start, stop and restart the burp suite.

1. Starting a Service

To start burp suite as a service go to Linux terminal as a root user and just use the following command.

root @ kali:service burpsuite start

This will start the service and you can check it using the ps command.

2. Stopping a Service

Stopping a service will completely abort everything that service is dealing with. So always, be careful while stopping a service as any unsaved data will be lost. Now use the following command to stop the service.

root @ kali:service burpsuite stop

You can check using ps command where you will not see anything related to burpsuit service.

3. Restarting a Service

Restarting a service just reboots everything about a particular service. Data will be lost and new service arises all on its own.

root @ kali:service burpsuit restart

This can be used when any service is struck or stops abruptly. Now in this below section we will use the Apache web server and MySQL to explain how services can be useful for a hacker. This is a very basic and introductory level of abusing services. If you are an efficient hacker, you will understand hundreds of services and will try to learn about them in time and time to be a professional.

Now let us start exploring these below services.

1. Apache Web server:

Apache is a famous web server that is being used by several hosting companies for deploying their web services. It is a well known open source web server that is well structured and of good security.

We will use this apache web server to learn a few things that can help us as a hacker.

Step 1: Starting Apache

Apache webserver can be started using the following command. Normally in windows and Hosting environment there will be a GUI that lets us start the Apache web server. But in Linux we need to enter the following command as a root user.

root @ kali: service apache start

This will start the web server in the background, which can be accessed from the localhost. You can check if everything is going well or not using ps command.

Step 2: Accessing the local host

Now after starting the server you can go to your local host address that is http://127.0.0.1 using your browser to access apache. You will be welcomed with an apache page that asks your permission to show the default page.

Step 3: Modify the webpage

Now for a practical example, modify html file to your desired and save it using any text editor. After few seconds come back to localhost and refresh. Boom! You can see the modified webpage. This confirms that service is being run on the background.

How an apache web server can help hackers?

Programmers to create a local host website during development phase usually use Apache web server. This can be linked with WAMP to further expand it with Php or MySQL servers. However, hackers can use it to learn about loopholes in websites without being blocked or banned. Hackers can also use Apache web server applications like Vulnerable App to expand their hacking skills. Almost every Hackathon program use the Apache web server for making their Hacking boxes.

Logging system

Being a hacker, you will certainly visit networks with high-level protection and maintained by hardworking security engineers. And if with all your skills you have exploited the system. After the attack, obviously a forensic investigation will take place and will try to find how an attack has been planned and executed. Everything of this investigation will be based on logfiles that you have left while exploiting the system.

Linux unlike windows is not vulnerable to exploits and attacking's because it has good logging system that records everything the user does. But some smart hackers use different techniques to make themselves undetectable by reading logfiles. We will explain in detail about how hackers need to develop skills to manipulate the logging system.

Rsyslog

rsyslog is a definite daemon program that takes care of log files to be created in the UNIX or Linux system. Every Linux distribution uses different techniques to deploy log files. Arch Linux uses a different process unlike Debian rsyslog function. As we are discussing about kali Linux that is a

Debian system we will continue with rsyslog explanation along with few examples. To know more about rsyslog we need to open its configuration file with any text editor. Please try to find syslog using find command and open it using your favorite text editor. And when you have successfully opened it please go through it and find Rules section. You will find some bizarre text like the following.

kern.* -var/log/kern.log

This is where log instructions are given to the Linux kernel. When we look at it thoroughly, we will find a basic command that log functionality uses. It is as the command shown below.

facility.priority action

We need to describe these three things in detail to get a thorough overview about the concept.

1. Facility

Facility is something, which is being logged. For example, mail designates about the mail system. There are few that comes under this category as explained below.

a. mail

This explains about the mailing system that is present in kali Linux. This precisely says that mail usage is being logged

b. user

All user related instructions or functions comes under this category.

c. kern

All messages that deals with the kernel comes under this category

d. lpr

All messages that deals with the inbuilt printing system comes under this.

2. Priority

If the facility describes which messages to log, priority decides on what to log. There are different types of messages that can be used to a better logging system. We will describe some of them below.

a) debug

This is used to log the things that happen as it is.

b) warning

This is used to log things that work but can go wrong.

c) info

This is used to log about normal information that exists. This can also be used to log date and time.

d) error

This can be used if something badly goes wrong while doing a work in Linux.

3. Action

This is quite simple to understand than the rest. It just means that the logs should be sent into this particular category. We may manually assign folder but it's better to leave them, as it is to go to var folder for better management. We will give some example destinations that logs are sent normally

Kernel files:

These are normally sent to /var/log/kernel . You can just go to the directory and open the log file using leafpad to analyze them. Now as we have learned everything we will just look at an example that deals with all of this.

mail.warning /var/log/warning

This precisely means that mail system warning message logs will be sent to /var/log/warning path.

Automatically clean logs

Log files can make up a lot of mess if you use them extensively. We need to make a strategy to keep how many logs depending on the time interval. However, we can use logrotate function in kali Linux to configure few functions that can help us clean log files.

Open logrotate.conf file and modify the text file to create your own log system according to your own necessity.

How to spoof log files?

You might wonder being a hacker how people get rid of tracking when they attack any target host. Luckily, Linux provides few functions, which can help us to spoof log files that is to modify them in a way such that network administrators cannot detect what happened during the attack. This process is called shred. We will explain about this process in detail in the below section.

Step 1:

Shred function just fills the log data with randomly generated UTF-8 code in the logged data again and again to make it as unusable data. To check shred function just click the below command in the Linux terminal as a root user.

root @ kali: shred

Step 2:

To make any file into unusable shred file you need to call the shred command with the file name. That's it. With a single click, all your data will be made into a difficult data that cannot be read or understood by anyone. The command is as below:

root @ kali: shred (insert file name here)

root @ kali: shred desktop/kalishred.txt

Step 3:

There is a special function in shred command that can help you shred the file as number of times you needed to be. But the only negative thing to worry about this is when you try to shred a file by 20 times the time taken will increase exponentially. So always listen to your senses when trying to shred a file multiple times. -n command describes the number of times function.

Command is shown as below:

root @ kali : shred -n 20 /desktop/kalishred.txt

There is also another way to make logging stop. When you have control over system as a root user, you can simply disable the service by using the following command. We can use three commands start, stop and restart for this service.

a) start

This starts the logging function allover again.

root@kali: service rsyslog start

b) stop

This stops the logging function in a split of a second.

root@kali: service rsyslog stop

c) Restart

This will first stop the logging function and will start again as a new variable.

root@kali: service rsyslog restart

Automating tasks with job scheduling

As a hacker, the most important skill you need to learn is to automate things. Whenever you attack a system or exploit a system, you need to get ready with a ton of things that will automate things for you. An automated backup or automated deletion of logfiles everything needs to be done for a better productivity and results. In this section, we will discuss in detail about automating tasks using kali Linux.

crontab

Crontab is a function that is available in kali Linux that will let us schedule an event or job for a particular time. We can enter the data from minutes to years to start a crontab task.

root @ kali : crontab

Click -help to check the functions of the crontab in detail.

Scheduling a backup task

Backup is one of the essential thing to do whenever you are dealing with an important data. When data is backed up, it can be used as an alternative if there is any leakage or corrupt in data. So administrators always prefer backing up the data.

But it is a difficult and boring task to backup manually every day. So we can create an automatic backup with the following command.

00 1 18,28 ** backup/desktop/backup.sh

Here first 00 stands for the top of the hour. And ** to any day of the month.

Crontab shortcuts

Below we will display a few shortcuts that are used in crontab automatic task scheduling.

1. @yearly

This will make the task to run once a year.

2. @ weekly

This will make a task to run once in a week

3. @ midnight

This will make a task to run at midnight every day.

Starting tasks at startup with rc

While startup certain scripts start their tasks automatically using rc scripts. This will help them prioritize in the process and will give good results. If you are willing to add a service to start automatically on a startup, you can use the following command.

root @ kali : update-rc.d servicename enable/disable

Protecting you with TOR and VPN

It is obvious that the most important thing for any hacker is his anonymity. Now days due to restrictions of Government and constant spying had made people to find alternate options to maintain anonymity like TOR and VPN. Before going to learn how to maintain your anonymity in Kali Linux, we will have a good explanation about all the options we have for securing ourselves in this matrix world that is all connected.

Why Anonymity matters?

Imagine if your country has blocked your internet access to social networking during riots and all of your people want to use it for better communication. You can do with a VPN or

TOR bundle and not are detected. However, tracking can be done in any other way if they want to. But make sure to follow this for some better peace. In the below section we will learn about anonymity services that has different uses.

What is a proxy server?

Proxy is a middle man between you and server that you are trying to reach. Imagine if you want to deliver a package from New York (your place) to Colorado (Server place). Instead of going and giving the package all by your own, you will ask your friend to deliver it. Here your friend acts a proxy for you. This is how the proxy server works.

There are many proxy servers like Socks4, http, https and Socks5.

How a hacker can use proxy server?

When doing a password attack you will normally be blocked by the website due to too many requests. In these situations, you can use a bunch of free proxies to randomly occupy the proxy address and attack the login page. This is a famous technique called cracking that is used by novice hackers to get an access into the system.

What is a VPN?

A VPN is a quite common advertisement that you might have used while watching ads in YouTube. A virtual private network abbreviated as a VPN acts like a middle man but delivers your request in encrypted form to the server in such a way that the server can't identify you. And when the server sends you the response it again encrypts it and sends towards you. Imagine this example to get a better understanding of how a Vpn works. Imagine that you want to deliver a Love Letter to your classmate. But you don't want any other person to read it other than your best friend. So, you write a Letter in quite a different way that no one can understand and sends by your friend to your classmate. Remember that your friends know how to read it. He will decrypt it to her and she will send a response in the same way. This is basically how a VPN works. In the next section, we will describe about how internet communication works and will give a practical example that will let us understand the fact that Anonymity is a must.

How the internet works?

Every internet connected device has an IP address that can be easily tracked using different techniques by the government.

When u send an email or surf internet without any Anonymity services, you are just being a product to Tech giants like Google. They will collect a lot of information from you and will sell you as adds to the businesses. Apart from that, every movement of yours will be tracked and can help them create new products.

Normally when we click on an URL the packet that contains your request will also contain the IP addresses of both yours and the server that you are trying to reach. In the communication process, it will travel through different routers called hops before reaching its final destination. When a packet is travelling, it can be easily sniffed and can be used to acquire information about you. For an example, use traceroute command to check how many hops that a particular website takes as below.

root @ kali: traceroute bing.com

You will get an output that shows the number of routers it needs to travel to reach the final destination. When the packet is travelling, anyone can sniff it and can attain sensitive information about you and your request.

What is TOR?

Concerned with security of Internet few independent security researchers has developed a network called TOR network that will encrypt the hop we are going through. TOR basically makes your request go through its servers all the while making your data encrypted and untraceable. This will dramatically increase the security of your system. But remember that this may make your networking slow as it needs to travel between encrypted servers. But when you are trying to attack a target host, it is best to use TOR network. To access TOR as a command line interface you can enter the following command.

root @ kali : tor service start

This will start the TOR bridge circuit for you and will make every request that is going on from your system to travel through TOR servers to reach destination server. You can also use TOR project bundle that consists of browser to use it for your daily purposes. A good thing about TOR browser that nothing of your information is tracked.

Is TOR the safest?

Unfortunately, you can't fully depend on TOR because there are rumors that some of TOR servers belong to NSA organizations. If at all your packet travels through one of their hops, your information can be easily retrieved. So, try to use it with Sock5 proxies so that you can never be tracked. In the next section, we will explain about proxies in detail. Proxies are the middle man and can be used for secure and safe communication. They are even extensively used for password attacks.

Kali Linux uses proxy chains a networking utility to manage proxy services in the operating system. We will learn about in detail in the next section.

a) Basic command

root @ kali : proxychain < rules here> < arguments here>

b) With proxychain we can proxy whatever service or process we want to. This will just an ip address on its top.

root @ kali : proxychains nmap -sV -Pn 192.232.2.1

c) You can set the proxies in proxychain configuration file and can use it to rotate whenever possible. You can find free proxies form many websites online. You can even buy premium proxies for a less rate in many markets.

d) Open website with a proxy in a browser This is a special command and automatically opens a webpage in a browser with desired proxy address. Command is shown below.

root @ kali: proxychains chrome www.bing.com

e) By default, if you add more than one proxy in the configuration file it will automatically move between the servers. They are used by different proxy chaining methods. The first one is dynamic chaining and the second one is random chaining.

(i) Dynamic chaining: This will help us to connect the web using chained proxies that are in an order. All the proxies are connected according to the order that they are placed in the configuration file.

(ii) Random chaining: This will help us to connect to the webservices using proxy chains and all the proxies are connected randomly as in the configuration file.

A little more about the Virtual private network

We discussed before about the functionality of a VPN in detail before. Before choosing, a good VPN try to look at the number of servers and countries it is offering. Some VPN services work slowly due to their latent proxy chaining methods. A Vpn can not only be used as an advanced proxying service but can also be used by organizations and universities to have off campus authorization easily. Services like Shibboleth does this for International universities. Nordvpn, Hma pro Vpn are the best virtual private networks that we can recommend because they delete the log files automatically and will be no chance of getting trace your activities.

Encrypted mail:

Free email services like Gmail and yahoo work well and gives us high storage facilities. But we are often vulnerable because our email data remains unencrypted and can be easily obtained by sniffing or other techniques that malicious hackers use. So to get rid of this try to use mail services like protonmail for a small price to make all your all mail encrypted. This is how we can protect ourselves from the tracking and become a hacker that everyone wishes to be.

CHAPTER 5:

WEB HACKING

In Previous chapters, have discussed a lot about Linux along with hacking and tricks that will help you achieve good results if you can work hard by expanding your knowledge as you go on. In this chapter, we will take quite a practical view of the side and discuss about web application hacking with the help of a tool named Burp suite. Burp Suite is one of the most famous hacking applications that can help us manipulate the tokens and by automatic scanning. In the later sections, we will describe about the Burp suite and its functionalities in detail.

Why web applications matter?

Now days in Internet every website is using webservices and has developed quite a large number of applications that can be vulnerable to attacks from malicious users. Also, web applications like PayPal can be an important target for hackers for huge theft of money. So web applications have a huge scope of vulnerability testing and fixing them. What is

Burp suite? Burp suite is a proxy interception tool that intercept every request from the browser and provides you to analyze tools that can manipulate the requests in a way that you can find vulnerabilities present.

How to install?

Burp Suite is a software that does not need to be installed. After the download is complete, it can be enabled directly from the command line. But Burp Suite is uses Java language development and the runtime depend on the JRE and requires a Java runtime environment in advance. However, in kali Linux it is preinstalled and can be found in the web application tools tab.

Configuring Burp in the Browser

1) IE settings Open IE Options -> Connections -> LAN Settings -> Check the use of proxy server for LAN -> Enter the address 127.0.0.1 and Port number 8080 (These are burp suite default assignment proxy address and port, you can make the corresponding changes)

2) Firefox settings And IE similar arrangement. Open Firefox-> Press alt to display the navigation bar-> Click Tools->Click

Options->Select Advanced- > Network in the newly opened about:preferences and at this point we will see the setting options of the Firefox connection network.

Then click on Settings, in the pop-up connection settings dialog box, find " http proxy", fill in 127.0.0.1 , Fill in port as 8080 , and finally click OK to save the parameter settings to complete the Firefox proxy configuration.

3) Chrome settings In the address bar, type chrome://settings/ to find "Settings", click on the bottom to display the advanced settings, then follow the above basic steps. If you want to capture using your phone, we can make the following settings.

1. The computer and the mobile phone are connected to the same network segment, which can be connected to a WIFI or a WIFI software (360wifi, cheetah, etc.) by the computer.

2. View the local IP through the ipconfig command. In the burpsuite, choose to create a listener with the same ip as the local ip. Pick a port that is not used.

3. Next, connect the phone to WIFI, choose to use the proxy, set the host name to the same as above, set the port to the same as above, and then you can capture the phone.

Basic use of burp proxy

a) Forward: This can be used to transfer the data that is being monitored.

b) Drop: This can be used to discard the data that is being used

c) Intercept on/off: This is a basic switch function that can decide whether intercept should be done or not

d) Action: provide function options

After the client and server intercepted by Burp Suite interact, we can view the entity content, header, request parameters and other information of the request in the message analysis tab of Burp Suite.

RAW:

In Main display, we can view Web RAW format request. The request comprises of an address, HTTP protocol version, host header, browser information, the acceptable content type, character set, coding, Cookie and so on. We can perform this test on the server side by manually modifying this information.

Params:

The view mainly displays the parameter information of the client request, the parameters including the GET or POST request, and the cookie parameters. The infiltrator can complete the penetration test on the server side by modifying these request parameters.

Headers:

The information displayed by the view is similar to that of Raw, except that it is more intuitive and friendly in this view.

Hex:

The view shows the binary content of Raw. You can modify the contents of the request through the hex editor.

Note: Messages intercepted by Burp proxy can be modified as needed in the Fitter (filter)

All messages flowing through burp proxy will be recorded in http history. We can view the transmitted data content through the history tab, test and verify the interactive data. At the same time, we can right-click to pop up the menu and send the content to other components of the burp that are processed.

Comment:

Add a comment to the intercepted message. In a penetration test, you usually encounter a series of request messages. For the sake of distinction, you can add a comment on a critical request message. The function of Highlight is similar to the Comment function that is, highlighting the currently intercepted message so that other request messages can be distinguished.

Optional parts Options

From the interface point of view, there are mainly the following major sections

- Client request message interception (This can be used to intercept client requests)

- Server-side return interception (This can be used to intercept server responses)

- Server returns message modification (This is used for response modification)

- Regular expression configuration (This can be used to match and replace)

- Other configuration items (Can be used for Miscellaneous purposes)

Use of the burp target

The Burp target component mainly consists of a site map, a target domain, and a target tool. This Help penetration testers had better understand the overall status of the target application, which target domains are involved in the current work, analyze possible attack surfaces, etc.

Target domain setting:

Application scenario

1. Limit the display results in the site map and Proxy history

2. Tell Burp Proxy what requests to intercept

3. What does Burp Spider crawl?

4. Which scope security vulnerabilities are automatically scanned by Burp Scanner

5. Specify the URL in Burp Intruder and Burp Repeater

Site Map

In a penetration test, the results of the history browsing through the browser in the site map will be automatically presented in the site map. The left side of the Site Map is the URL of the visit. According to the level and depth of the website, the tree shows the structure of the entire application system and the URL of other domains. The right side shows the list of the URLs that are accessed, and which URLs are accessed right now.

What is the request and response content, each has a detailed record? Based on the tree structure on the left, we can select a branch to scan and grab the specified path.

Use of the Target tool

1) Get the site map manually:

1. Set the browser proxy and the burp proxy to make it work properly.

2. Turn off the intercept function

3. Manually browse the web At this time, the target will automatically record the site map information. One of the advantages of manually obtaining a site map is that we can control the access content autonomously according to our own needs and analysis, and the recorded information is more accurate. Compared with automatic crawling, it takes longer. If the product system that needs to be infiltrated is a large-scale system, then the energy and time required to operate the system's function points in turn will be paid to the penetration testers. Very big.

2) Site comparison

A tool for dynamic analysis of sites, we often use it when comparing account permissions. When we log in to the application system and use different accounts, the account itself is given different permissions in the application system, then the function modules, contents, parameters, etc. that the account can access are all different.

It can help the penetration tester to distinguish well.

In general, there are three main scenarios:

1. The same account, with different permissions, compare the difference between the two request results.

2. Two different accounts with different permissions, comparing the difference between the two request results.

3. Two different accounts with the same permissions, comparing the difference between the two request results.

Step by step instruction:

1. First we right click on the site that needs to be compared to find the site comparison menu "Compare site maps"

2. Since the site comparison is between the two site maps, we need to specify Site Map1 and Site Map2 separately during the configuration process. Normally, Site Map 1 defaults to the current session. Click [Next] as shown.

3. At this point we will enter the Site Map 1 settings page. If it is a full site comparison, we choose the first item. If we only compare the features we selected, we will select the second item. Click [Next]. If the entire site is compared and you don't want to load other domains, we can check to select only the current domain.

4. Then there is the Site Map 2 configuration for Site Map 2 We also have two ways, the first is before we have preserved Burp Suite site records, and the second is a request to re-occur as a Site Map2. Here, we choose the second way.

5. If the second method is selected in the previous step, enter the request message setting interface. In this interface, we need to specify the number of concurrent threads for communication, the number of failed retries, and the time between pauses.

6. After setting up Site Map 1 and Site Map 2, the request message matching settings will be entered. In this interface, we can filter the matching conditions by URL file path, Http request mode, request parameters, request header, and request body.

7. Set the request matching condition, and then enter the response comparison setting interface. In this interface, we can set what we specify to be compared

8. If we used to compare the whole station and choose to re- create it as Site Map2, the progress of the data loading will be prompted during the interface loading process.

If there are fewer links involving function requests, it is very go to the comparison interface.

3) *Attack surface analysis*

Step by step instructions:

1. Right click to find [Engagement tools] (interactive tool), click on analyze Target to use.

2. In the pop-up analysis interface, we can see an overview of dynamic the URL of, static the URL of, parameter 4 views.

3. The overview view mainly shows the current site dynamic URL number, the number of static URLs, the total number of parameters, and the number of unique parameter names. Through this information, we have a rough understanding of the overall status of the current site.

4. The dynamic URL view shows all dynamic URL request and response messages, similar to other tools. When you select a message, the details of the message are displayed below.

5. The parameter view consists of upper, middle and lower parts. The upper part is the parameter and parameter

count statistical area. You can sort by the number of times the parameter is used, and analyze the frequently used parameters. The middle part is the parameter usage list, and the record is the usage record of each parameter is used; the lower part is the detailed information of the request message and the response message during a certain use.

When using the attack surface analysis function, it should be noted that this function is mainly used to analyze the request URL in the site map. If some URLs are not recorded, they will not be analyzed. At the same time, in actual use, very few sites use pseudo-static. If the requested URL does not contain parameters, the analysis cannot be distinguished, and can only be analyzed as a static URL.

4) The use of burp spider

Burp Spider's features are primarily used for large-scale application testing, which helps us quickly understand the structure and distribution of the system in a short amount of time.

Spider control

The Spider control interface consists of two functions, the Spider state and the Spider scope. In addition to displaying the current progress, transmission status, request queue and other statistics, the Spider status also has a Spider Run / Pause button and an Empty Queue button, which are used to control whether the Spider is running and the data management in the queue. The Spider scope is used to control the scope of the Spider's crawl. From the figure, we can see that there are two control methods, one is to use the Target Scope in the previous section, and the other is user-defined. Here custom configuration scope Target Scope of exactly the same configuration, a specific method, please use the parameters Target Scope configuration.

Spider option settings

The Spider option settings consist of six parts: the crawl settings, the crawl proxy settings, the form submission settings, the application login settings, the spider engine settings, and the request header settings.

5) *Use of the Burp scanner*

Burp Scanner's function is mainly used to automatically detect various vulnerabilities in web systems. We can use Burp Scanner instead of manually performing penetration testing of common vulnerability types on the system, so that we can put more energy into those that must be manually Verify the vulnerability. Scanner's scanning methods are divided into two types, active scanning and passive scanning.

1. Active scanning (Active Scanning)

When using the Active Scan mode, Burp sends a new request to the application and verifies the vulnerability through the payload. The operation in this mode generates a large amount of request and response data, which directly affects the performance of the system and is usually used in non-production environments.

It has a good scan effect on the following two types of vulnerabilities:

1. client vulnerabilities, like XSS, Http header injection, operation redirection.

2. server-side vulnerabilities, like SQL injection, command line injection, file traversal.

For the first type of vulnerability, Burp will submit the input field when it detects it, and then parse it based on the response data. During the detection process, Burp will modify the basic request information, that is, modify the parameters according to the characteristics of the vulnerability, and simulate the behavior of the person to achieve the purpose of detecting the vulnerability. For the second type of vulnerability, detection is generally more difficult because it occurs on the server side. For example, SQL injection may return a database error message, or it may be nothing. In the detection process, Burp uses various techniques to verify the existence of vulnerabilities, such as induction time delay, forced modification of Boolean values, and comparison with the results of fuzzy tests, and has reached a highly accurate vulnerability scan report.

2. Passive scanning (Passive Scanning)

When using passive scan mode, Burp will not resend new requests. It only analyzes existing requests and responses. This is safer for system detection, especially if you are authorized to access it. Generate a detection of the environment. In general, the following vulnerabilities are easily detected in passive mode:

1. The submitted password is unencrypted plaintext.

2. Unsafe cookie properties, such as missing HTTP Only and security flags.

3. The scope of 3 cookies is missing.

4. cross-domain scripting and site reference leaks.

5. Form values are automatically populated, especially passwords.

6. SSL protected content cache.

7. Directory listings.

8. The response is delayed after the password is submitted.

9. Insecure transmission of 9 session tokens.

10. Sensitive information leaks, such as internal IP addresses, email addresses, stack traces and other information leaks.

11. Unsafe View State configuration.

12. Error or non-standard Content-type directives.

Although the passive scanning mode has many shortcomings compared to the active mode, it also has the advantages that the active mode does not have. In addition to the above-mentioned detection of the system is safer within the scope of our authorization, when testing a certain business scenario when each test leads to a certain aspect of the business, we can also use the passive scan mode to verify the existence of the problem and reduce the risk of testing.

Scanner's specific steps

1. Passive scanning

   In the Burp suite Professional Edition, the passive scanning of all sites intercepted by default, we can see in the site map tab under the Target, the situation shown in the figure, the two red boxes respectively indicate the vulnerability of a site And specific details of a vulnerability. We can modify the scope of work in Scope to facilitate our targeted analysis work. You can also adjust our scanning strategy in the Live Scanner tab under Scanner, such as canceling passive scanning of all sites.

2. Active scanning

We can actively scan a site in a variety of ways, the operation is very simple. After an active scan in one way, we can go to the graph tab to view the progress of the scan. The scan shows that the scan has been completed. Four problems were found and a total of 513 responses were received. After double-clicking on this record, we can view the detailed vulnerability scan report.

6) Use of Burp Intruder

Working principle:

Intruder obtains different request responses by modifying various request parameters based on the original request data. In each request, Intruder usually carries one or more payloads (payloads), performs attack replay at different locations, and obtains the required feature data through comparison analysis of response data.

Application scenario:

1. Identifier enumeration Web applications often use identifiers to reference data information such as users, accounts, assets, and so on. For example, username, file ID, and account number.

2. Extract useful data in some scenarios, rather than simply identifying valid identifiers, you need to extract some other data with a simple identifier. For example, you want to get the nickname and age of all users in the personal space standard through the user's personal space id.

3. Fuzzy testing Many input-type vulnerabilities, such as SQL injection, cross-site scripting, and file path traversal, can be used to test applications by submitting various test strings through request parameters and analyzing error messages and other exceptions. Manual execution of this test is a time consuming and cumbersome process due to the size and complexity of the application. In this scenario, you can set up Payload to automate the fuzzing of web applications with Burp Intruder.

Test steps:

1. Verify that the Burp Suite is properly installed and started up properly, and that the browser's proxy settings are completed.

2. Enter Burp Proxy tab, turn off the proxy blocking.

3. Historical log (History) sub-tab and look for potential problems request logs, and right-click menu, sent to the Intruder.

4. Be Intruder tab, open the Target and Positions sub-tab. At this point, you will see the request message sent in the previous step.

5. Because we understand that the basis of the Burp Intruder attack is to set up a certain amount of attack payload Payload at the location specified by the original information around the original request information just sent, and send a request to obtain a response message through Payload. By default, all request parameters and cookie parameters are set to add payload

6. Click clear to clear the default load (if needed), circle the parameters that need to set the load, click add

7. When we open the Payload subtab, select the Payload generation or selection strategy, and select " Simple list" by default. Of course, you can also select other Payload types by drop-down or add them manually.

8. Then click start attack to launch the attack. At this time, the burp will automatically open a new interface containing the results of the execution of the attack, http

status code, length and other information. We can also select one of the communication messages to view the details of the request message and the reply message.

In many cases, in order to better indicate whether the response message contains the information we need, usually before the attack, the Options option is configured, and the most used is regular expression matching (Grep - Match). Or we select the filter in the Results tab to filter the results. At the same time, the columns shown in the results tab can be specified; we can set them in the menu columns.

Finally select the column we need, click the save button to save the attack results. You can also set the contents of the saved pair.

Payload type and processing

A total of 18 kinds

1. Simplelist:

    By configuring a string list as a payload, you can also manually add a string list or load a string list from a file.

2. Runtimefile:

The specified file, as corresponding Payload on the location Payload list. At runtime, Burp Intruder will read each line of the file as a Payload.

3. Customiterator:

A powerful Payload with a total of 8 placeholders. Each placeholder can specify a simple list of Payload types. Then, according to the number of places, a Cartesian product is generated with each simple list of Payload to generate a final Payload list.

For example, the value format of a parameter is

Username@@password, the steps to set up this Payload are: location 1, select Usernames . Next, specify location 2, enter the value @@ and finally specify location 3, and select Passwords. When we start the attack, the generated Payload values are as shown:

4. String replacement:

As the name suggests, this type of Payload is to replace the predefined string to generate a new Payload. For example, the predefined string is ABCD. After setting the replacement rule as shown in the figure below, the value of AB will be enumerated to generate a new

Payload. Then A will be replaced by 4 and B will be replaced by 8

5. Case replacement:

The generation rules are: 1 NO change 2To lower caser 3To upper case 4To Propername initial capitalization, other lowercase 5To ProperName initial capitalization, others do not change

6. Recursivegrep:

This Payload type is mainly used to extract valid data from the server side. It is necessary to extract data from the server response as Payload, and then replace the location of the Payload to attack. It comes from the original data response message, based on the original response, the Payload may option (the Options configuration) Grep rule, then according grep to extract data attacks can occur. For example, I set the server-side Eagle Id as the new Payload value in grep extract. After clicking OK, the payload settings are completed. When an attack is launched, Burp analyzes each response message. If the value of EagleId is extracted, then A second request occurs as Payload.

7. Illegal unicode encoding:

   The payload itself is replaced with the specified illegal Unicode encoding in the payloads, and one or more payloads are generated from these Payload lists. This payload can be useful when trying to avoid input validation based on pattern matching.

8. Character block:

   This type of Payload refers to the use of a given input string to generate a specified size of the character block according to the specified settings, in the form of a string of the specified length. It usually uses a boundary test or a buffer overflow.

9. Number type:

   * Depending on the configuration, a series of numbers is generated as Payload.Type indicates whether to use a sequence or a random number. From indicates what number to start with, to indicates what number to cut off, * Step indicates how much the step size is. If it is a random number, how many is activated, indicating how many random numbers are generated.

   * Base indicates whether the number is in decimal or hexadecimal form. * Min integerdigits indicates what

the smallest integer is, and Max integer digits indicates what the largest integer is. * If it is 10 decimal, the Minfractiondigits represents the minimum number of digits after the decimal point, Max fraction digits represent up to several decimal numbers.

10. Date Type:

Depending on the configuration, a series of dates is generated. The format can be selected from the sample format provided by Burp, or it can be customized.

11. Brute forcer:

This type of payload generates all the payloads of a specified length that contain a specified character set, usually used to generate dictionary entries. Character set represents the data set of the generated dictionary, and characters are extracted from this data set for generation. Min length represents the minimum length of the generated Payload, and Max length represents the maximum length of the generated Payload.

12. Nullpayloads:

This payload type produces a Payload whose value is an empty string. In the case of an attack, the same request is required to be executed repeatedly, and this Payload is very useful in the absence of any modification of the original request. It can be used for a variety of attacks, such as sequence analysis of cookies, application layer Dos, or keep alive session tokens for use in other intermittent trials.

13. Characterfrobber:

This type of Payload is generated by modifying the value of the specified string at each character position in turn, each time incrementing the ASCII code of the character on the original character. It is typically used in test systems that use complex session token components to track session state. When you modify the value of a single character in a session token, your session is still processed, and then it is likely that the token is actually not used to track your conversation.

14. Bitflipper:

The original value of the preset Payload is modified in order according to the bit. Setting Options: Operation: Specify whether to perform bit flip on the payload raw data, or specify the value for bit flip. Format of original data refers to whether to operate on the textual meaning of the original data, or should it be treated as ASCII hexadecimal Select bits to flip refers to the position of the Bit that is selected for flipping. You can configure to operate based on textual meaning, or flip based on ASCII hexadecimal strings.

15. Username generator:

This type of payload is mainly used for automatic generation of user names and email accounts. For example, I set the original value to 123456789 @qq.com, and then execute the payload generator, and the generated payload value is as shown in the figure.

16. ECB blockshuffler:

This type of Payload is a Payload generator based on the ECB encryption mode, which verifies whether the application is vulnerable by changing the location of the packet data.

17. Extension-generated plugin:

This type of Payload is based on the Burp plugin to generate the Payload value, so you must install the configuration Burp plugin before use, register an Intruder payload generator in the plugin, which can be called here.

18. Copy another payload:

This type of Payload copies the parameters of other locations to the Payload location. As a new Payload value, it is usually applied to request messages with multiple parameters.

Its usage scenario may be:

1. Two different parameters need to be used. The same value, for example, when the user registers, the password setting will be entered twice, and the value is exactly the same, you can use this Payload type.

2. In a request, the value of one parameter is based on the value of another parameter generated by the script in the front end. This Payload type can be used. Its setting interface and parameters are relatively simple, as shown in the following figure, where the index value of the Payload position is the value of the Payload set in the figure.

Attack mode

1. Sniper (only one payload location can be used)

Use a set of payloads to replace the text marked by § at the payload location (without the text marked by § will

144

not be affected), requesting the server side, usually used to test whether the request parameters are vulnerable.

2. Battering ram

It uses a single Payload collection, which in turn replaces the text marked by § in the Payload position (the text without the § flag will not be affected), requests the server side, and the difference with the sniper mode is that if there are multiple parameters The Payload values used are the same when both are Payload position markers, while the sniper mode can only use one Payload position marker.

3. Pitchfork grass

It can use multiple sets of Payload collections to traverse all Payloads at each of the different Payload flag locations (up to 20). For example, if there are two Payload flag positions, the first Payload value is A and B, and the second Payload value is C and D, then when the attack is launched, two attacks will be initiated, and the first used Payload. A and C respectively, and the second used Payload are B and D respectively.

4. Clusterbomb

It can use multiple sets of Payload collections, traversing all Payloads in turn at each of the different Payload flag positions (up to 20). The main difference between it and the grass-fork mode is the product of the Payload data Payload group that is executed. For example, if there are two Payload flag positions, the first Payload value is A and B, and the second Payload value is C and D, then when the attack is launched, a total of four attacks will be initiated, the first use of Payload. A and C respectively, the second used Payload are A and D respectively, the third used Payload are B and C respectively, and the fourth used Payload are respectively B and D.

Optional options

1. Request message header is provided

   This setting is mainly used to control the header information of the request message. Update Content-Length header if checked, Burp Intruder adds or updates the Content-Length header for each request to the correct length of the HTTP body of the request. This feature is usually used to attack the body of an HTTP request that inserts a variable-length Payload into the template. If the correct value is not specified, the target server may return an error and may respond to an incomplete request. Or you may wait indefinitely for a request to continue receiving data. Set the Connection: Close, if checked, indicates that Burp Intruder adds or updates a connector with a value of "closed" in each request message, which will be executed more quickly.

2. RequestEngine - mainly used to control the burst intruder attack

   Number of threads ----- concurrent threads Number of Network retries ------ ON failure to a network failure, when the number of retries Pause before ---- retry pause interval before retry Throttle between---- requests request delay StarTime----- start time to happen

3. GrepMatch Extract

   result items from response messages If it matches, it is marked in the new column added in the attack result, which is convenient for sorting and data extraction. For example, in a password guessing attack, such as "password is incorrect" or "login successful", you can find a successful login; in the test SQL injection vulnerability, scanning messages containing " ODBC" , "error" and other messages can identify vulnerable parameters.

4. GrepExtract

These settings can be used to extract useful information from the response message. For each item configured in the list, Burp adds a new result column containing the text from which the item was extracted. You can then sort the data extracted by this column (by clicking the column header) command. This option is useful from application data mining and can support a wide range of attacks.

5. GrepPayloads

These settings can be used to extract whether the response message contains the value of Payload

6. Redirection (Redirections)

These settings are mainly used to control the attacks a Burp how to handle the redirection We can modify the parameters of the packet here to perform message verification analysis of the request and response.

7. How to use the burst sequencer

A tool for detecting the randomness quality of data samples usually used to detect whether the access token is predictable, whether the password reset token is predictable, etc., and the data sample analysis by Sequencer can well reduce the forgery of these key data. Risks of.

Steps for usage:

1. Confirm the correct operation of the burpsuite, open the interception

2. From the history log of burpproxy, look for tokens or similar parameters (cookies, etc.), right click to pop up the context menu, click send to sequencer

3. Go to the live cature panel of burpsequencer, select the record you just sent and click configure to configure the token or parameter to be analyzed.

4. In the parameter configuration dialog box that pops up, select the value of the parameter and click ok to complete the parameter setting.

5. Click select live capture to start the parameter value acquisition.

6. When the total number of parameter values captured is greater than 100 , click [pause] or [stop], and then you can perform data analysis, and click [Alylyze now] to analyze the randomness of the data.

7. After the analysis is over, you can see the various charts of the analysis results.

8. We can also save the acquired data, and load the parameters from the folder for data analysis the next time we use it. - Click savetokens to save the data

9. When using again, directly in the manual load, click load ... to load the data

Optional settings

The purpose of analyzing the option settings is mainly to control the token or parameters, what kind of processing needs to be done during the data analysis, and what type of randomness analysis.

It consists mainly of token processing (Token Handling) and token analysis (Token Analysis).

- token handling, the main control token in the data analysis, how to be processed

- shorttokens at start / end means that if the tokens generated by the application are of variable length, then these tokens need to be populated before data analysis to facilitate statistical testing. You can choose whether to fill in the starting position or the end of each token. In most cases, filling at the starting position is the most appropriate.

- Padwith means you can specify the characters that will be used for padding. In most cases, a numeric or ASCII hex-encoded token, padded with a " 0" is most appropriate.

- Base64-decode before analyzing indicates whether base64 decoding is performed in data analysis. If the token uses base64 encoding, you need to check this box.

Token Analysis

Mainly used to control the type of random analysis of data, we can select multiple analysis types, or you can enable or disable each character type level and byte level test separately. Sometimes, after performing a preliminary analysis with all analysis types enabled, some analysis types are disabled to better understand the characteristics of the token, or to isolate any unusual characteristics exhibited by the sample.

Count:

Analyzes the distribution of characters used in each position within the token. If it is a randomly generated sample, the distribution of characters used is likely to be roughly uniform.

Transitions:

Analyze changes between consecutive symbols in sample data. In the case of a randomly generated sample, the character appearing at a given position is a change in the next flag that may also be passed through any of the characters used at that position.

The following settings are byte level tests used to control data analysis. In byte-level analysis enabled, each token is converted into a set of bytes, and the total number of bits determined by the size of the character set at each character position is determined.

FIPS monobit test

The test analyzes the allocation of 0 and 1 at each bit position. If it is a randomly generated sample, the number of 1's and 0 's is likely to be approximately equal. The FIPS test formal specification assumes a total of 20,000 samples. If you want to get the same results as the FIPS specification, you should..

FIPS poker test

The test divides the bit sequence into four consecutive, non-overlapping packets, then derives four numbers, calculates the number of times each number has 16 possible digits, and uses a chi-square check to evaluate the distribution of the numbers. If the sample is randomly generated, the distribution of this number may be approximately uniform.

FIPS runs tests

The test divides successive bit sequences having the same value into segments at each position, and then calculates the length of each segment to be 1, 2, 3, 4, 5, and 6 and 6 or more. If the samples are randomly generated, the length of these segments is likely to be within the range determined by the size of the sample set.

FIPS longruns test

This test divides successive bit sequences with the same value into segments at each position, counting the longest segment. If the sample is randomly generated, the number of longest segments is likely to be within the range determined by the size of the sample set.

Correlation test

Comparing the entropy between a token sample with the same value for each location and a short token sample with a different value for each location to test for any statistically significant relationship between values in different bit positions within the token. If the sample is randomly generated, the value at a given bit position is also likely to be accompanied by one or a zero at any other bit position. Thus, we ended this book with a bang after going through burp suite and quite a lot of information about web hacking. Now just make experiments with lot of examples and try to attack as many websites as possible.

CONCLUSION

Thank you for making it through to the end of Book Title, let's hope it was informative and able to provide you with all of the tools you need to achieve your goals whatever they may be. The next step is to make these things apply in real practical hacking life. After understanding the intrusion methods commonly used by hackers, it is not realistic to plan separate protection strategies for these methods. Therefore, users can only master the common protection strategies of personal computer security to ensure that the computer is in a relatively safe environment.

Common PC protection strategies include: installing and upgrading anti-virus software, enabling firewalls, preventing Trojans and viruses, sharing folders and regularly backing up important data. The emergence of viruses has caused huge losses to computers on the Internet. These viruses can cause the system to fail to operate normally, and the system will be formatted and data will be formatted.

In order to prevent the harm caused by these viruses, users need to install anti-virus software on the computer and turn on real-time monitoring. In addition, due to the improvement of virus production techniques and means, new viruses are constantly appearing, so users need to upgrade anti-virus software in time, so that anti-virus software can prevent new viruses in the Internet. A firewall is a method of separating a computer's internal network from an external network. In fact, this is an isolation technique. A firewall is an access control scale that is executed when two internal and external networks communicate.

It allows users' licensed computers and specific data to enter the internal network, preventing hackers on the external network from accessing and attacking themselves to the maximum extent. In order to prevent Trojans and viruses from invading the Internet, first of all, do not download unidentified software and programs, select a reputable download site to download the program, and then put the successfully downloaded software and programs in addition to the system partition. Other partitions and need to use anti-virus software to scan downloaded programs before opening.

In addition, do not open e-mails and attachments of unknown origin to avoid the invasion of mail viruses or bundled Trojans. Even if you download the attachment that came with the message, you need to scan it with anti-virus software. On the Internet, some hackers use "phishing" methods to scam, such as creating fake websites or sending e-mails containing fraudulent information, thereby stealing online banking, online payment tools, credit card accounts and passwords, and stealing funds from the account. . In order to prevent phishing, users must make sure that the URL of the private information they enter is the real URL, not the phishing website. Do not enter it at will. In the LAN, when users share files, there will be software vulnerabilities, and hackers will detect these vulnerabilities. Therefore, users must set the access password when setting up a shared folder. Unshared should be canceled as soon as sharing is not required. In addition, when setting up a shared folder, users must make the shared folder read-only and do not set the entire disk partition as shared. The importance of data backup is unquestionable, and no matter how tightly the computer's preventive measures are made, it cannot completely prevent unexpected situations. If a hacker is fatally attacked, although the operating system and application software can be reinstalled, important data cannot be reinstalled, and only rely on daily backup work. Therefore, even if you take very strict precautions, don't forget to back up your important data at any time and be prepared.